How Will It Really End?

OTHER TITLES FOR THE YOUNG

In addition to *How Will It Really End?* Solid Ground Christian Books is pleased to offer several other books especially intended for young people and young Christians. Some are listed below:

Addresses to Young Men by Daniel Baker

Advice to a Young Christian by Jared Waterbury

My Brother's Keeper: Letters to a Younger Brother by J.W. Alexander

A Manual for the Young: An Exposition of Proverbs 1 – 9 by Charles Bridges

Opening Up Ephesians for Young People by Peter Jeffery

Scripture Biography for the Young by Thomas H. Gallaudet

The Scripture Guide by J.W. Alexander

Whatsoever Things Are True: Discourses on Truth by J.H. Thornwell

The Workman: His False Friends & True Friends by Joseph P. Thompson

Young Lady's Guide by Harvey Newcomb

Young People's Problems by J.R. Miller

Youth's Book on Natural Theology by Thomas H. Gallaudet

HOW WILL IT REALLY END?

Eschatology for Young People

Steve Daniels

SOLID GROUND CHRISTIAN BOOKS
Birmingham, Alabama USA

Solid Ground Christian Books
PO Box 660132
Vestavia Hills AL 35266
205-443-0311
mike.sgcb@gmail.com
www.solid-ground-books.com

HOW WILL IT REALLY END?
Eschatology for Young People

Steve Daniels

First Solid Ground Edition in November 2011

Cover design by Borgo Design
Contact them at borgogirl@bellsouth.net

ISBN- 978-159925-316-9

A very special thank you to the kind reviewers whose insight and encouragement helped move this project across the finish line. Your literary works are a blessing to God's people.

To my sons who were among the first reviewers and to Melissa, who patiently caught my countless grammatical errors (and helped fix them)--you are blessings to me.

Finally, thanks to all the Friday night Bible study friends who forced me to grapple with these issues—each night together has been a blessing.

Steve Daniels is a professional forester with a private forest and land management company with responsibility for long term planning, forecasting, and technical services. Steve has been married to Melissa for 20 years, and they have been blessed with six sons and one daughter. Steve and Melissa are members of University Church in Athens, GA (they live nearby in Watkinsville, GA). He has led a Bible study for adults and "aspiring" adults for which the book material was developed. He has several prior publications in his professional field (forestry). His personal interests include camping, canoeing, fishing, the English Puritans, and southern African missions.

TABLE OF CONTENTS

TABLE OF CONTENTS

PREFACE

As I write these words, the world continues on pretty much the way it has for centuries. While this may seem to be such an obvious statement that it hardly needs comment, it is not. In recent months a well-known personality on Christian radio has been predicting the return of Christ on May 21, 2011, and the end of the world on October 21, 2011. To the delight and derision of the watching world, both dates have now passed without incident.

This is not the first failed "prophecy" by this individual, nor his last. He previously predicted that the end of the world would occur in 1994. Sadly, he stuck with his prediction–maintaining that a *spiritual* judgment did indeed take place in May and the end of the world would still arrive in a few short months. Now his second date has come and gone and he is silent about his most recent failed prediction. Such speculation brings ridicule on the church and on the cause of Christ. Worse perhaps, if possible, this type of "prophecy" flatly contradicts the clear teaching of Jesus, "But concerning that day or that hour, no one knows, not even the angels in heaven, nor the Son, but only the Father" (Mark 13:32). To claim otherwise is to attempt to nullify the words of Christ and claim knowledge that he says we do not have. Despite the contorted attempts to reconcile end-of-the-world predictions with this verse, failure and embarrassment are inevitable.

Other individuals focus speculative energy on the fact that the ancient Mayan calendar ends in 2012 and thus so must the world. We are actually asked to believe that a pagan, idolatrous culture had knowledge that all the prophets, apostles, angels, and Jesus himself did not possess. "But concerning that day or that hour, no one knows, not even the angels in heaven, nor the Son, but only the Father."

One would expect some misguided individuals, even small numbers of uninformed Christians perhaps, to occasionally fall for a deception. What is troubling, however, is the large numbers of followers such individuals attract and the way many will continue to believe them despite the repeated failures of their predictions. Many of their followers have abandoned earthly property and have sent this individual significant sums of money to support his work. God's people, above all others, should know better than to believe claims so out of accord with the clear teaching of Scripture. These claims are speculative. They are not grounded in a careful, sober-minded study of God's Word. This book is an attempt to set forth the clear teaching of Scripture on a number of themes relating to the return of the Lord and the end of the world. If it helps Christians (especially the younger readers) avoid being taken captive by false teaching, it will have served its purpose.

October 2011

INTRODUCTION

Have you ever wondered how it all ends? How the world and everything in it comes to a close? Have you thought much about what happens to people when they die? Do they live again? Are they gone? Gone forever? Are they happy, or sad? Are things better, or worse? Does the earth simply wear out or wind down like a clock? Or perhaps you may think the world goes on forever and without an end? I could understand you thinking that way. It's gone on pretty much the same for as long as anyone can remember. But the Bible tells us this present earth does end. In fact, the Bible tells us something about all these questions. It tells what happens to people when they die. It tells what will happen to the earth someday. It explains *why* people die and what happens to them when they do. It explains *why* we see the earth afflicted with earthquakes and storms and plagues. It explains that these things, wars and fighting and suffering, are to be expected. The Bible helps us understand these things and more, much more.

Eschatology is the study of the last things that happen on this present earth, including the end of the world and the return of Jesus Christ. Some of the Bible's teachings on the subject of end times are difficult to understand—but some are quite easy. One thing is clear, however, and it is that the Bible focuses our attention on the return of Jesus Christ. No sooner had Jesus left earth the first time to go back to heaven than a couple angels told the apostles he will return (Acts 1:11). The apostle Paul encourages Christians to look for "the blessed hope and glorious appearing of our great God and Savior Jesus Christ" (Titus 2:13). And John, perhaps the last living apostle, assures us that every eye will see Jesus when he comes again, and that he will return as a conquering king (Revelation 1:7, 19:16). The Bible is full of passages like these!

3

Page after page, book after book we are encouraged to think about Jesus returning to earth. Verses about "end times" and the second coming of Jesus are some of the most common themes, or teachings, found in the New Testament. Unfortunately, they are often overlooked or misunderstood.

This book is designed to provide a general overview of what the Bible teaches about the end–the end of this world–the end of this life as we know it–and about the life to come. Of course, knowing this will impact how we live now. It should encourage us to think more about heaven and about the consequences of our life on this earth. Most importantly though, I hope this book will make you think more about the return of Jesus. That is the most important. The goal of this book is to make you think about *and look forward to* the return of Jesus! Paul identified Christians as people who "long for" or "eagerly wait for" Jesus' coming (2 Tim. 4:8). It is one of the most important and common themes in the Bible–and children as well as adults should spend more time thinking about it. Christians today think much about Jesus' first coming, often called the first advent. This is especially so around the Christmas holiday. However, the New Testament has far more to say about the second coming, or second advent, than the first. Passages about the second coming touch on many themes. The second coming is frequently used in passages warning non-Christians to prepare for a day of wrath. Paul uses the promise of Christ's return to comfort grieving Christians who have lost Christian loved ones to death. We are encouraged to lay up treasure in heaven, to be zealous for good works–in anticipation of our reward that Christ brings when he comes. Those who suffer persecution because of their faith in Christ are promised relief when Christ returns to completely defeat our common enemies (including Satan). Far from being a specialized study for experts, a study of Christ's second coming is a major theme throughout the Bible.

CHAPTER 1

He is Coming Back!

One of the most important truths taught in the Bible is that Jesus will return. He is coming back to be with his people whom he has by no means forgotten. In Acts 1:11, mentioned above, Jesus had just returned to heaven. Some disciples were standing and looking upward into heaven. Two angels suddenly appeared and said, "Men of Galilee, why do you stand here looking into the sky? This same Jesus, who has been taken from you into heaven, will come back in the same way you have seen him go into heaven." It does not get clearer than this. The angels say to the disciples, "He will come back." The Bible repeats this teaching many, many times. All the New Testament writers write about some aspect of the second coming. Paul, Peter, and John seem to mention it the most. Of course, Jesus himself spoke about his return to earth on a number of occasions.

In this chapter we will look at three of the most important words used to describe the second coming of Jesus. These words were written in Greek, but in English they are usually translated as "coming," "revelation," and "appearance." We'll look at them one at a time.

When you think of the word "coming," you think of someone arriving, of someone who wasn't present before but is now on the scene. Someone who has been absent is arriving. Perhaps you haven't seen some favorite relatives for a long time and now you learn they are on their way. You would naturally be excited. The coming of Jesus is like this, but so much more. You might think of the President of the United States walking into Congress for an important speech. Many people come and go from the room without much notice. Congressmen, aides, reporters, and invited guests all move in and out of the room and nothing seems to change. Then the President appears. An officer bangs a gavel on his desk, an announcement is made in a loud voice, music may play, people stand, heads turn–the mood grows serious and respectful. This begins to illustrate the importance and seriousness with which the Bible treats the coming of Jesus. Notice how the disciples framed their question to Jesus about his second coming. "What will be the sign of your *coming* and of the end of the age?" (Matthew 24:3) They believed, correctly, that the second coming of Jesus marked the end of the age–that is, it marked the end of the world in their thinking. This showed how important the idea was in the minds of the apostles. We should carefully note Jesus' answer, "For as lightning that comes from the east is visible even in the west, so will be the coming of the Son of Man" (Matthew 24:27). The key points in this comparison to lightning are its suddenness and its incredible power. It's easy to see. When it comes, you know it. We see that the coming of Jesus is much more than the coming of some other person. My coming into the room would not be compared to lightning.

Jesus then continued his answer about the time of his coming and the end of the age in verses 36-39. He said,

> No one knows about that day or hour, not even the angels in heaven, nor the Son, but only the Father. As it was in the days of Noah, so it will be at the coming of the Son of Man. For in the days before the flood, people were eating and drinking, marrying and giving in marriage, up to the day Noah entered the ark; and they knew nothing about what would happen until the flood came and took them away. That is how it will be at the coming of the Son of Man.

Jesus compared his return to the days of Noah. Recall that Noah preached about the coming flood, but people did not believe him. They doubted. They no doubt mocked Noah and his family. They carried on with their lives (eating, drinking, and marrying) as if things would go on the way they always had. Then the flood came and took them away. They were caught by surprise–completely unprepared for what happened. Noah spoke the truth but none would believe. Jesus' point is that his coming is just as certain as the flood. People hear about it but don't believe the truth. Those who do not believe and heed the warnings will be caught just as surprised and unprepared as those who were shut outside the ark. They will suffer an awful fate. If something is so certain, why would people not believe?

We will look at one of the numerous places where the apostle Paul uses the word "coming." Paul uses it in his second letter to the church at Thessalonica when he describes how Jesus deals with the Antichrist–that most wicked of men who purposely sets himself up in open opposition to Christ and all things related to Christianity. (We will talk more about the Antichrist in a later chapter.) He says, "and then the lawless one will be revealed, whom the Lord Jesus will kill with the breath of his mouth and bring to nothing by the appearance of his coming" (2 Thessalonians 2:8). Jesus does not have to struggle and strain to defeat this enemy–he is victorious simply at his coming! His coming is full of splendor. It is majestic. Heads will turn. He will have everyone's full attention. His coming is not like a mere man walking into a room. His coming ends the age. His coming will be like lightning lighting up the sky. His coming will slay his opposition. The Bible is clear: *he is coming, and it will not be missed!*

The second word we will look at that the Bible frequently uses to describe the return of Christ is the word "revealed," or as it is often used, "revelation." The word revealing brings to mind that has been out of sight that suddenly becomes visible; it comes shockingly into plain view. When automobile makers want to present a fancy new car to the public, they may cover it in a cloth or curtain, and then suddenly yank the curtain away–revealing the shiny new car! People gasp. They are frequently very impressed! There is often an element of surprise and suddenness. In some cases a revealing could lead to fear. Remember when Joseph made himself known to his brothers in Egypt? They had treated him wrongly by selling him into slavery. Now he was a high ranking official in Egypt and they were coming to him to buy much-needed food. When he announced who he was, you could say he revealed himself. The Bible says they were terrified (Genesis 45). There was suddenness about his announcement. They were surprised, and they were afraid.

The last book in the Bible is titled "Revelation," or sometimes "The Revelation," after the first two words of the first verse. It is about the revelation, or revealing, of Jesus Christ. It will be breathtaking. All will see it. No one will miss it! It will bring an end to sin and to the suffering of God's people. It will bring a fateful end to the wicked. It is much more than the revealing of a new car–and even more shocking than Joseph's surprise announcement to his brothers. It is such a momentous event that words alone cannot describe it–the book of Revelation uses pictures for things too great for words.

This word, "revealed," occurs elsewhere in the New Testament. We'll look at a few more instances. Notice what Paul writes to the Corinthians:

> Therefore you do not lack any spiritual gift as you eagerly wait for our Lord Jesus Christ to be revealed. He will keep you strong to the end, so that you will be blameless on the day of our Lord Jesus Christ (1 Corinthians 1:7-8).

There can be no doubt Paul is expecting Jesus to come at the end as he says. Remember the question the apostles asked Jesus in Matthew 24:3 about the sign of his *coming* and of the end? Paul is referring to the same point in time–it's the end–the day when Jesus comes for the second time. Here though, Paul speaks of it not as coming but as a *revealing*. Christ will keep you strong until the end, until he is revealed. Paul apparently thinks it is important to be blameless on the day Jesus is revealed. Why might that be? As we shall see in a later chapter, Jesus will judge the wicked on that day. Christians can take comfort in Paul's words. Note that Paul says to the believers in Corinth, "You do not lack any spiritual gift," and "He will keep you strong to the end." God is able and willing to take care of those who are his!

God not only keeps his children strong and blameless until his return, but he punishes our enemies. Notice what Paul says elsewhere,

> God is just: he will pay back trouble to those who trouble you and give relief to you who are troubled, and to us as well. This will happen when the Lord Jesus is revealed from heaven in blazing fire with his powerful angels. He will punish those who do not know God and do not obey the gospel of our Lord Jesus Christ (2 Thessalonians 1:6-8).

God notices the trouble that wicked people cause his children. He will pay back the trouble they cause. This ought to be comforting. As Christians, we do not need to pay back the wrong that others commit towards us. God takes care of that. Notice when this happens–when he is revealed from heaven in blazing fire and with angels. He gives comfort and relief to his people, and vengeance and trouble to those who oppose him. He is revealed in a manner like no other.

The third word the Bible uses to describe the return of Jesus to earth is the word "appearance." We use this word in many different ways in everyday speech. We speak of spring appearing. We speak of the sun appearing on the horizon. We speak of a player or performer appearing on a stage or ball field. As with the other words we described above (coming and revealing) the word "appearing" takes on a much more powerful meaning when applied to Jesus. Concerning Jesus' first coming to earth, the Bible says Jesus appeared and destroyed death and brought life and immortality to light through the gospel (2 Timothy 1:10). Does anyone else appear and do these things? Yet that is exactly what Jesus did. He overcame death by dying and rising again. He brought life to others by his sinless life and by shedding his own blood. His first appearance on earth changed everything–it changed even life and death.

Do we expect his second coming to be any different? Do we expect less of him in the future? Paul teaches that Jesus' future appearance is no less shocking. In his future appearing Jesus will "judge the living and the dead" (2 Timothy 4:1). In expectation of this appearing Paul tells Timothy to "preach the word." People need to hear the message of the gospel–the message that they can find forgiveness in Christ–but they must find it before he returns. Those who receive the message of the gospel and find the forgiveness to be freely had in Christ need not fear the coming of the Judge. They should look forward to his appearing–they will receive an award! Paul states, "Henceforth there is laid up for me the crown of righteousness, which the Lord, the righteous judge, will award to me on that Day, and not only to me but also to all who have loved his appearing" (2 Timothy 4:8). There is a day when Jesus appears to punish the wicked and reward the righteous who long for his appearing. Do you long for his appearing as the verse says? His children, the righteous ones, long for his appearing. To long for something means to have a have a strong desire for something to occur, to have great expectation. God's people have this desire. I urge you, children, to ask yourself honestly if you long for his coming. Does it matter to you? Have you thought about his appearing and what it means for your soul?

Application: Consider the grand terms the Bible uses to describe the return of Jesus. It will be accompanied by signs; it is compared to lightning; he will be revealed with blazing fire and with angels; it will be a day of judgment. Some will receive a most unpleasant surprise–like those left outside the ark the day the flood began. But for others it will be the most blessed day imaginable–the day they see their Lord face to face. They will "long for his appearing" (2 Timothy 4:8). What kind of day will it be for you?

CHAPTER 2

When Will He Return?

The question of when Christ will return has been the subject of much debate among Christians for many years. It has been discussed since Jesus walked the earth. We will need two chapters to answer this challenging question. In this chapter will discuss the way the Bible presents time–all of the time from Biblical days until the end of the world. The concept is very simple–the Bible refers to the time in which we live as "this age." The Bible also indicates that after this age is complete, we move into "the age to come." "This age" and "the age to come" summarize the Biblical structure of time. It is extremely important to have a good understanding of this concept. The Bible also teaches that this age ends and the next one begins at the second coming of Christ. Again, this is surprisingly simple. This age continues until Christ returns. His return begins the age to come. However, the question of when this will happen is not as clear. That will be the subject of the next chapter. For now, let's look at what the Bible has to say about this age and the age to come.

One of the clearest illustrations of the division of time into two ages can be found in a pair of verses that can be described as parallel verses. Parallel verses are ones that say essentially the same thing but with slightly different language. *Parallelism* is frequently used in the Bible, often within a single verse. You see this in many places in the Psalms and Proverbs. As an example, consider Proverbs 19:5: "A false witness will not go unpunished, and he who breathes out lies will not escape." Notice that the proverb says the same thing twice but with different words. In the first half the sinner is referred to as a "false witness," while in the second as one who "breathes lies." One might wonder what or who a false witness is. By comparing the unfamiliar term with the familiar one, you can conclude that a false witness is one who tells lies. Notice in the first half of the proverb this person is said to not go unpunished, in the second half he is warned that he will not escape. To not go unpunished and to not escape are parallel truths.

As mentioned, parallelism occurs between or across multiple verses, even in different books of the Bible. Many examples are found in the words of Jesus. The words and deeds of Christ were recorded by four different writers. They often gave accounts of the same event or sermon, but with different words. By comparing the different accounts from the different witnesses, we gain a better understanding of his words and actions than we would otherwise with only one account. In a modern-day example, consider the way policemen investigate an automobile accident. They interview different witnesses. One witness may have been walking and watched the accident from the sidewalk. He will have one perspective. Each of the drivers will have a perspective. Someone watching the wreck from a second story window will have a bird's eye view. By comparing these different, or parallel, perspectives from different witnesses, the police gain a better understanding of what happened and why it happened. This is what we mean by parallel accounts (or parallelism) in the Bible. Many words or sayings that may be difficult to understand in one part of the Bible are often explained more clearly in another. By comparing one Scripture to another Scripture we gain a better understanding of what God is telling us.

A couple parallel passages concerning the two ages we have been discussing occur in Matthew and Mark. Consider these two verses together:

> And whoever speaks a word against the Son of Man will be forgiven, but whoever speaks against the Holy Spirit will not be forgiven, *either in this age or in the age to come* (Matthew 12:32, emphasis added).

Truly, I say to you, all sins will be forgiven the children of man, and whatever blasphemies they utter, but whoever blasphemes against the Holy Spirit never has forgiveness, but is guilty of an eternal sin—for they were saying, 'He has an unclean spirit' (Mark 3:28-30, emphasis added).

Based on the context, people were saying Jesus derived his power from a demon, perhaps even from Satan himself. Mark refers to a person who "speaks against the Holy Spirit." Matthew uses the word "blaspheme." We can therefore conclude that the word blaspheme concerns speaking against the Spirit. To our point, Jesus is warning that these people may be committing the most serious of all sins—one that will never be forgiven. Notice the emphasized words in the Matthew verse. These individuals will not be forgiven "in this age or in the age to come." This is the exact language we have been discussing. If we stopped reading here, we might be left with the impression that there could be many ages, that while this person may not be forgiven in this age or even in the one to come, perhaps they would have some hope of forgiveness in some undisclosed age after the one to come. Perhaps we could argue they might receive forgiveness in some age between "this age" and "the one to come." Here is where we see the value of the parallel verse. Notice Mark says that the person committing this sin *never* has forgiveness and is emphatically guilty of an *eternal* sin. The double emphasis of "never" and "eternal" sin makes perfectly clear that there is no hope either between this age and the next, or after the next age. This age and the age to come cover all time—they exclude all hope of this wicked person being forgiven. As this book unfolds we will see why division of time is so important—the Bible says Jesus returns between this age and the one to come. This division is important to any discussion of his second coming.

A second passage illustrating this same division of time occurs in Mark. Notice what Mark says about the rewards those who follow Christ will receive.

Jesus said, "Truly, I say to you, there is no one who has left house or brothers or sisters or mother or father or children or lands, for my sake and for the gospel, who will not receive a hundredfold now *in this time*, houses and brothers and sisters and mothers and children and lands, with persecutions, *and in the age to come* eternal life" (Mark 10:29-30).

Notice that Jesus is saying those who follow him in this life will receive a hundredfold in this time (or age) and in the age to come, "eternal life." The "age to come" is the age where the Christian receives eternal life. Recall in the previous verses the blasphemer was guilty of an eternal sin in the age to come. The age to come is the final age–the age where one receives either eternal life or eternal punishment. This age is the one we now live in–the age in which some commit sins against the Holy Spirit and some make sacrifices to follow Christ. There can be no age after the eternal one–and these verses do not leave any room for an age in-between. There is the time we live in, and the time after that is eternity. If we sacrifice lands and houses and must leave family members to follow Christ we will receive a hundredfold now–in this age–and eternal life in the age to come.

The apostle Paul teaches that the name of Christ is the highest and best name of all. As he does so, he also shows us that he too believes in the division of time into two and only two ages. Notice how he frames his argument:

> [God] worked in Christ when he raised him from the dead and seated him at his right hand in the heavenly places, far above all rule and authority and power and dominion, and above every name that is named, not only in this age but also in the one to come (Ephesians 1:20-21).

Paul says Christ was seated in heaven above every name that is ever named–not only in this age but in the one to come. Paul leaves no possibility of a name higher than Christ's. If there were some other age in between the two ages, or some age after the age to come, there would exist the possibility of a higher name. Paul excludes this possibility. He says Christ is seated above "all" rule and authority and above "every" name. By these words Paul excludes all names and rulers in this age and the one to come. In his thinking, "this age" and the age "to come" clearly cover "all" and "every" name conceivable. He leaves no other time for a rival name. There is no greater name during this age, after the next age, or in between the two. His is above all.

The deceitful Sadducees provided another opportunity for Jesus to discuss this issue. They had come to Jesus with a trick question. Interestingly, it concerned the resurrection and what heaven would be like.

> There came to him some Sadducees, those who deny that there is a resurrection, and they asked him a question, saying, "Teacher, Moses wrote for us that if a man's brother dies, having a wife but no children, the man must take the widow and raise up offspring for his brother. Now there were seven brothers. The first took a wife, and died without children. And the second and the third took her, and likewise all seven left no children and died. Afterward the woman also died. In the resurrection, therefore, whose wife will the woman be? For the seven had her as wife." And Jesus said to them, "The sons of *this age* marry and are given in marriage, but those who are considered worthy to attain to *that age* and to the resurrection from the dead neither marry nor are given in marriage, for they cannot die anymore, because they are equal to angels and are sons of God, being sons of the resurrection" (Luke 20:27-36, emphasis added).

The Sadducees were wrong in not believing in the resurrection. They attempted to catch Jesus in a trick question. The question was designed to show that Jesus' teaching on the resurrection was false and illogical. Jesus, of course, recognized their trap for what it was and turned it around and caught them in it. He used the occasion to show that they did not know what they were talking about. In doing so, he also taught us something new about the age to come. In the trick question, the Sadducees asked about a fictitious woman whose husbands kept dying before she had any children. Under Jewish law this circumstance required the dead man's brother to marry her and father children on behalf of his brother. In their twisted thinking each husband kept dying–then finally the woman died. They wanted Jesus to tell them whose wife she would be in the resurrection. Jesus illustrated their lack of understanding about heaven and the resurrection when he informed them that "the sons of this age marry" but those worthy of "that age" do not. Again, there are clearly two ages in Jesus' thinking. In one age they marry–in the other they do not. There is no in-between state. In addition to confirming what we have said about the two ages, Jesus adds the fact about marriage. The two ages are quite different in this regard–we marry in this current age–but we do not marry in the next age.

Jesus taught something else in this exchange about how the ages differ. Note how the basis of the trick question involved seven men and one woman dying. Jesus accepts the fact that people in this age die (he refers to the "resurrection from the *dead*"), but he corrected their thinking about the age to come–"for they cannot die anymore." Again, the two ages are quite different; in this present age people die, and in the age to come people do not. In this age death is common and expected; in the age to come it is impossible.

Interestingly, Jesus gives us yet more new information about the age to come. He offers us a clue as to how the age to come actually begins. He refers to those "worthy to attain to that age and to the resurrection from the dead." In this verse he *seems* to be saying that Christians enter the age to come at the "resurrection from the dead." We will see ample evidence in later chapters that this is in fact what the Bible teaches. Jesus answered their question so well that Luke informs us in verse 40 that they dared not ask him another one.

The final passage we will look at concerning this age and the age to come is the parable of the weeds and the wheat. You may have noticed that Jesus often spoke in parables, especially when he talked about heaven or the kingdom of God. Many people did not understand the parables immediately. Some never would. Others might figure them out after some time of reflection. In this particular case it seemed that few, if any, understood Jesus' story. The disciples later asked Jesus to explain it, which he did. This makes this parable particularly valuable as Jesus rarely explained his stories. As such, it provides an opportunity to test one's interpretive skills before reading Jesus' response. Matthew 13:1-9 contains the parable as it was told to Jesus' original audience. It would do you good to read it and see if you can understand it before reading further.

Jesus' explanation of the parable of the weeds and the wheat is provided below:

> Then he [Jesus] left the crowds and went into the house. And his disciples came to him, saying, "Explain to us the parable of the weeds of the field." He answered, "The one who sows the good seed is the Son of Man. The field is the world, and the good seed is the sons of the kingdom. The weeds are the sons of the evil one, and the enemy who sowed them is the devil. The harvest is the close of the age, and the reapers are angels. Just as the weeds are gathered and burned with fire, so will it be at the close of the age. The Son of Man will send his angels, and they will gather out of his kingdom all causes of sin and all law-breakers, and throw them into the fiery furnace. In that place there will be weeping and gnashing of teeth. Then the righteous will shine like the sun in the kingdom of their Father. He who has ears, let him hear" (Matthew 13:36-43).

Here Jesus refers only to the "close of the age" without specifically using the phrase "the age to come." In the parable the wheat represents the "sons of the kingdom." The weeds represent "sons of the evil one," that is, the devil. The wicked and the righteous live and grow together until the close of the age. In God's judgment, where he is assisted by angels ("the reapers"), he sends the wicked into the "fiery furnace," while the righteous are gathered into the kingdom where they "shine like the sun." It should be fairly obvious that the fiery furnace and "shining like the sun" represent hell and heaven. We will discuss heaven and hell in later chapters. For now, it shall be sufficient to say that the two conditions following the judgment, shining like the sun or burning in a fiery furnace, are quite different conditions than are experienced in this age. They are qualitatively different. These new conditions begin with "the harvest" at the close of the current age.

Application: When Jesus returns, it marks the end of this age and the beginning of the age to come. At that time the wicked will be cast into the "furnace" and the righteous will "shine like the sun" with Jesus. The apostle Paul warns us in Titus 2:12-13 to live upright and godly lives "in this present age" as we "wait for the appearing of the glory of our great God and Savior Jesus Christ." Those who live this way and truly look forward to his appearing can expect to "shine like the sun." Those who do not should expect to face the furnace. Which will it be for you?

CHAPTER 3

Isn't there More to this Age?

By this point you may well be wondering if it can really be as simple as two and only two ages. The short answer is yes, it is that simple. But yes, there is more to it as well. Perhaps you have thought that somehow the first coming of Christ should play into our outline a little, that it must oversimplify things a bit to leave Jesus' life on earth completely out of the picture. Surely our outline should recognize so vital a component as the first coming of Christ. Any outline of history must somehow represent a significant section or division attributed to Christ's first coming within this age. After all, there would be no second coming without a first coming. It must be conceded that our outline, the simple two age outline set forth in the last chapter, should be amended to account for such a critical event. However, we maintain that the two age structure is correct—we are simply adding a component to clarify and to make it more complete.

As we study the New Testament's teaching concerning this age and this world we live in, we see that this age and world are passing away; they are dying. The Bible presents the time in which we live as the "last days." If there are "last days," then there surely must have been days before the last one! In this chapter we will explore what the Bible teaches about these last days. We will discover the main characteristics of the last days when they began and what came before them. We will also see that the last days are still part of the present age. Finally, we will see there is a Biblical contrast between the last days (plural) and the *last day* (singular).

Life on this planet will not continue forever in its present state. Notice what John says concerning the world he lived in: "the world is passing away along with its desires, but whoever does the will of God abides forever" (1 John 2:17). Paul says something similar: "Yet among the mature we do impart wisdom, although it is not a wisdom of this age or of the rulers of this age, who are doomed to pass away" (1 Corinthians 2:6). Whether we think of our world as the physical planet we live on, or we think in terms of the "age" or time in which we live, it is passing away. This passing away began with the sin of Adam, which we will discuss below. However, we will see that the world entered a new phase of "passing away" with the first coming of Christ. The Bible teaches that with the first coming we entered the last days of this life and world. These last days are still part of this age–but they are different than the days that came before.

Peter declares this very clearly in his famous sermon on the Day of Pentecost:

> But this is what was uttered through the prophet Joel: "And in the last days it shall be, God declares, that I will pour out my Spirit on all flesh, and your sons and your daughters shall prophesy, and your young men shall see visions, and your old men shall dream dreams" (Acts 2:16-17).

The Holy Spirit had been poured out on believers on the Day of Pentecost as the prophet Joel had predicted. Some onlookers actually thought the people were drunk with wine. Peter, however, points out that they were full of the Holy Spirit and that this is the miraculous pouring out of the Spirit that marks the last days. Peter confirms that at this point in history the last days were in progress. The pouring out of the Spirit was associated with the first coming of Christ. You may recall that when Jesus left earth to return to the Father, he said he would nonetheless be with us (Matthew 28:20). How was he with us? He was not with us in his physical body, but he continued to be with us in his Spirit. Likewise, Jesus instructed the disciples to remain in Jerusalem and not begin their missionary duties related to the great commission until they received the Holy Spirit (Acts 1:4-5). This missionary activity was associated with the first coming. Jesus being with his people through his Holy Spirit, and his people obeying his direct command are marks of the last days. They began with the whole complex of events associated with the first coming.

Peter first tied the last days to the work of the Spirit on the Day of Pentecost. Later he ties them directly to the first appearing of Christ:

> ...knowing that you were ransomed from the futile ways inherited from your forefathers, not with perishable things such as silver or gold, but with the precious blood of Christ, like that of a lamb without blemish or spot. He was foreknown before the foundation of the world but was made manifest in the last times for the sake of you who through him are believers in God, who raised him from the dead and gave him glory, so that your faith and hope are in God" (1 Peter 1:18-21).

Here Peter refers to the "last times" but the difference does not change the point. It is the last part of the current age. The word is vague in that it does not indicate how many actual calendar days, weeks, or months are intended. That is not the point. His point is that the last major stage of God's unfolding plan has begun and is underway as of the first appearing of Christ, when he was "made manifest" according to Peter. Notice it is particularly tied to Jesus' blood, his role as a lamb, his being raised from the dead, and God giving him glory. It would be hard, even impossible, to say that any one of these by itself began the last days Peter refers to. However, they are undeniably all part of the one great first coming.

Finally, the writer of the book of Hebrews ties the last days directly to the work of Jesus Christ as God's messenger. He says,

> Long ago, at many times and in many ways, God spoke to our fathers by the prophets, but in these last days he has spoken to us by his Son, whom he appointed the heir of all things, through whom also he created the world (Hebrews 1:1-2).

In the last days God spoke to his people not through prophets, but directly through his Son. It is not the first time God spoke to man for the text says God spoke many times and in many ways before. Nor is this the first work of Christ, for the Bible says he was involved in creating the world. But what it does say is that it is indicative of the last days that God sent his Son to speak to us directly.

If we wanted to summarize what we have learned so far, we could say something like the following: "We are in the last days of this age, waiting for the age to come. The last days began with the set of events associated with Christ's first advent." We could diagram what we have stated so far as follows:

World passing away → Christ → last days begin → last day

This is an accurate summary of our conclusions so far but it leaves a couple of questions unanswered. First, one might naturally wonder when this age *began*. Second, one could understandably ask when will this age *end?* The second question will be discussed in the rest of this chapter. The first question is relatively easy and can be addressed now.

The things we have learned about this age give us a clue as to when it began. Recall the trick question asked of Jesus about the woman who had seven husbands who all died before having children? Recall how Jesus answered:

> And Jesus said to them, "The sons of this age marry and are given in marriage, but those who are considered worthy to attain to that age and to the resurrection from the dead neither marry nor are given in marriage, for they cannot die anymore, because they are equal to angels and are sons of God, being sons of the resurrection" (Luke 20:34-36).

This passage is rich in terms of answering our questions about the beginning and ending of this age. Jesus teaches that the sons of this age die. We know that dying began at the first sin, at the fall of Adam in the Garden of Eden. Therefore we can conclude that this age had to have been in progress at least as early as the first sin.

The parable of the tares and the wheat (Matthew 13:36-43) that we previously discussed also confirms this. The wicked and the righteous live together in the world in this age. This mingling of the righteous and the wicked began to take place with the first family; certainly Cain and Abel illustrate this principle.

Therefore we can conclude that nearly the entire time of man on earth, certainly since the fall, can be considered this age. Now we can amend our summary statement about what we have discussed so far. We might now say, "We are in the last days of the age that began with the sin of Adam, and are waiting for the age to come. The last days began with the set of events associated with Christ's first advent." We can summarize this statement as follows:

Adam's sin → world begins passing away →
Christ → last days begin → last day

Now we can turn our attention to the second question we asked about the last days, the one about when these days will end.

To begin to determine when this age ends we need look no further than the passage with the trick question concerning marriage that we just discussed. Look again at Luke 20:34-36 quoted above.

Notice Jesus said the sons of this age marry (and they obviously die–which was the basis of the trick question) but that those who attain "that age and the resurrection from the dead neither marry nor die." We pass from an age when we can marry and can die to an age when we cannot marry and cannot die. We do this when we attain the resurrection. Do you see the value of the resurrection in this argument? This is the turning point, or you might say the door, the door to the next age when we can no longer die and we no longer marry. Notice what we can say now: "We are in the last days of the age that began with the sin of Adam, and are waiting for the age to come. The last days began with the set of events associated with Christ's first advent. The last days end with the resurrection of all the dead." Our summary is getting much more complete. If we dig a little deeper though, we can learn more about what happens at the end of this age.

Before we leave the topic of the last days we need to discuss one more related topic. You may recall from the Bible that it sometimes refers to the last *day* in contrast to the last *days*. As you know, the difference between singular and plural can have a big impact on the meaning of what someone says.

All the passages discussed above refer to the last days–the days we are living in–the days that began with the first coming of our Lord and will continue until the end. However, the Bible also speaks of *the* Last Day. The last days do not go on forever, there is a last day! Time and history lead to a climax.

We will look at this language in the book of John. Notice what he quotes Jesus as saying,

> And this is the will of him who sent me, that I shall lose none of all that he has given me, but raise them up at the last day. For my Father's will is that everyone who looks to the Son and believes in him shall have eternal life, and I will raise him up at the last day (John 6:39-40).

Twice in these two verses John records Jesus saying that he (Jesus) will raise his people on the last day. He will not raise them throughout the last days (plural); otherwise we would expect resurrections to be taking place on a regular basis all around us. On the contrary, Jesus will raise his people on the last day.

Interestingly, Jesus ties eternal life together with the raising up of his people. While Christians enjoy some of the benefits of eternal life at the moment they become followers of Christ, they physically enter eternal life at the resurrection on the last day. Eternal life is tied directly to the age to come. The last day marks the end of this age and the beginning of the age to come. Recall those who left everything to follow Jesus? They will "receive a hundredfold now in this time, houses and brothers and sisters and mothers and children and lands, with persecutions, and in the age to come eternal life" (Mark 10:29-30). Eternal life is a mark of the age to come. Recall the trick question Jesus was asked about marriage? Those who "attain to that age and to the resurrection from the dead neither marry nor are given in marriage, for they cannot die anymore, because they are equal to angels and are sons of God, being sons of the resurrection." The parable of the tares and the wheat teaches the same thing. Of course, there is a sense in which we can say that we have eternal life already. The point to understand here is that we will not fully enjoy all of its benefits until the age to come.

Returning to John 6:39-40, quoted above, we see Jesus emphasizing that the resurrection is on the last day. "No one can come to me unless the Father who sent me draws him, and I will raise him up at the last day" (John 6:44). And again, in the same chapter he makes the same point, "Whoever eats my flesh and drinks my blood has eternal life, and I will raise him up at the last day" (John 6:54). It is hard to escape Jesus' meaning–there will be a resurrection on the last day. Martha obviously understood this when she discussed Lazarus's resurrection with Jesus. Martha answered, "I know he will rise again in the resurrection at the last day" (John 11:24).

Jesus later adds something else that will happen on the last day. In John 12:48 he tells us that the judgment will be on the last day. "There is a judge for the one who rejects me and does not accept my words; that very word which I spoke will condemn him at the last day." At this point a little detective work is in order. Here Jesus indicates the judgment will be on the last day. Previously he said the resurrection would be on the last day. If both the resurrection and the judgment are on the last day they must both be on the same day! This may seem to be a very obvious conclusion but it is one that is often missed. It is a vital point if we are to understand the days we live in and how they will end.

We will explore these events and their timing in a later chapter–but for now this additional information helps us add a little more detail to the summary we've been working on. We may now say, "We are in the last days of the age that began with the sin of Adam, and are waiting for eternal life in the age to come. The last days began with the set of events associated with Christ's first advent and will end on the last day with the resurrection and judgment."

Application: The days we are living in will not continue forever. There will be an end, a last day. The Bible says that day will come suddenly upon those who are not prepared. And while these *are* evil days, full of sin and full of death, they are also very blessed days. These last days are the days with the Holy Spirit, days when the Son has spoken directly to us, and they are days of repentance. In these last days we have the golden opportunity to turn from our sins. On the last day it will be too late to turn from our sins. Some will find that last day to be the most blessed they have ever experienced. They will see the Lord Jesus face to face as did the apostles. Others, however, will see that last day as a day of painful judgment. When the last days end and the last day arrives, your destiny will be heaven or hell–forever. The Bible indicates there will be no in-between time, no in-between days to make peace with God. Think about this now, while it is still today. "Today, if you hear his voice, do not harden your hearts" (Hebrews 3:15).

CHAPTER 4

The Last Days–Already and Not Yet

At the end of the last chapter you were asked to think about whether the last day would be a blessed day for you or a dreaded day. You were encouraged to make peace with God while you live in this age, before the last day (singular!) arrives and it becomes too late. In these last days we are privileged to have the words of the Son spoken directly to his people. We are fortunate to have the Holy Spirit poured out for the benefit of God's children. We are fortunate to have marriage in this age. These are indeed good days.

But we were also reminded that this age is an evil age. Despite the blessings we enjoy, the last days of this age continue to be evil. The trick question about marriage asked of Jesus indicates that there is still death. The parable of the tares and the wheat indicate that the sons of the evil one continue to persecute the sons of God. This age is an age of spiritual darkness. Notice just a few of the many Biblical statements to this effect:

> The light shines in the darkness, but the darkness has not understood it (John 1:5).

> Because of the tender mercy of our God, by which the rising sun will come to us from heaven to shine on those living in darkness and in the shadow of death, to guide our feet into the path of peace (Luke 1:78-79).

> This is the verdict: Light has come into the world, but men loved darkness instead of light because their deeds were evil. Everyone who does evil hates the light, and will not come into the light for fear that his deeds will be exposed (John 3:19-20).

The darkness and evil are really nothing new. This age has always been an evil age. From the first sin of Adam until the day you are reading this it has been an evil age. But despite the evil, there has always been mercy on the part of God. At the beginning of this age, immediately following Adam's sin, God began hinting that there would be grace. He would come and crush the evil one (Genesis 3:15). He has been unfolding this grace throughout this age. This grace, however, was made clear in the last days. In these last days the Son appeared, the Holy Spirit was poured out on all who would believe, and God offered a taste of the age to come.

Curiously, these last days mark an overlapping of this age and the age to come. We still live in this age but we get a glimpse, a small taste, a preview of the age to come. You are familiar with the concept I'm referring to by the term "overlapping" even if you haven't given it much thought. Many reading these words are still children–but at the same time you are a young adult. You have some of the opportunities of childhood and some of the responsibilities of adulthood. You love the opportunities to play and experience relatively carefree days, and yet you probably look forward to driving, perhaps a first job, and maybe even marriage and starting your own family. Your childhood and your adulthood are overlapping. We have often told friends that we are not raising children–we are raising adults. That is certainly true in a sense, but to get to adulthood you must pass through childhood. You live now in childhood but your goal, or destination, is to be a responsible adult. Similarly, our goal and hopefully final destination is to be with God in heaven, to inherit the age to come. However, we must pass through this age to get there. In between, while living in this age, we get little tastes of the age to come. The two ages overlap.

Night and day seem to overlap a bit as well. You have noticed early in the morning, just as it is getting light, that you can see the sun and still see the moon and stars. Night is mostly over, but not quite, and the day is getting started but is not fully underway. Of course the reverse happens in the evening. It is a little dark and a little light at the same time. The dark and light overlap.

Many of you have been to the mountains or the beach. As we drive from our home to the mountains we begin to notice that after an hour or so the hills start getting a little steeper and taller. The engine labors more and more as it climbs. As we cross a bridge we notice the rivers are getting narrower and rockier. The types of trees change as well. We begin to see some tree species that grow in the mountains. We smell some of the smells common to the mountains (certain types of woods burning, flowers blooming). We begin to see signs for whitewater rafting and camping. But we are not in the mountains yet. We are in-between the flatter terrain that characterizes our state and the mountains that are our destination. However, the conditions all around us are part flat and part hilly. The trees are partly typical of the flat part of the state and partly typical of the mountains. The sights, smells, terrain, and activities are overlapping.

As it is with children and adults, night and day, and traveling across changing terrain, so it is in the spiritual realm in these last days. While we are stuck in this age, the last days afford considerable pleasures and opportunities that belong to the age to come. This chapter will look at a few of these benefits and see how this age and the age to come overlap each other. This is not a third age that is qualitatively different–it is still this age–with death, sin, and marriage–but we get a taste of the age to come.

We will begin with something John said in his first letter:

> Yet I am writing you a new command; its truth is seen in him and you, because the *darkness is passing and the true light is already shining.* Anyone who claims to be in the light but hates his brother is still in the darkness (1 John 2:8-9).

Just as it is true in our analogy with night ending and day beginning, so it is true in the spiritual realm. Here John is speaking of spiritual darkness and spiritual light. The darkness of sin and ignorance of God is passing away and the true light of God, the knowledge of Jesus Christ, is already shining in the world. It shone in the flesh with his first coming. But John's point is that the age of darkness and the age of light are overlapping–they are both occurring together. This age continues mostly as it has–full of evil–shrouded in darkness, but the age to come has pierced the darkness–like rays of sunlight finding holes in the clouds–and has begun shining in the hearts of some.

Paul makes the point concerning the new life of the child of God. In speaking to the Corinthians he said, "Therefore, if anyone is in Christ, he is a new creation; the old has gone, the new has come!" (2 Corinthians 5:17) Paul says we are a new creation and that the old has gone. He says this despite the obvious fact that we are still in our old bodies–our bodies that are wearing out in this age. In heaven we shall have new, perfect bodies that will never be spoiled by sin. However, when we become Christians our bodies do not immediately change. We keep the same broken bodies. We even continue to sin. What he means is that we have a new life in God–we are changed in such a way that we want to please God; we want to live for God. Pleasing God is something the old man, the non-Christian, had no desire to do. So we are new in that we have new desires. We are new in that our sin disturbs and grieves us when we used to enjoy it. But we still live with our old bodies. We still sin. Again, the old and the new live together. They overlap.

The writer to the Hebrews speaks very directly about those who actually taste the powers of the age to come. Read his inspired words:

> It is impossible for those who have once been enlightened, who have tasted the heavenly gift, who have shared in the Holy Spirit, who have tasted the goodness of the word of God and the powers of the coming age, if they fall away, to be brought back to repentance (Hebrews 6:4-6).

These are, to be fair, difficult verses. Some think the writer to the Hebrews is saying that it is possible to lose one's salvation. I personally do not think this is the case. I think he is speaking in hypothetical terms. However, what does seem clear is that he alludes to the fact that people in this age taste the Holy Spirit, the word of God, and *the powers of the coming age*. Even now, in this age, the powers of the age to come have broken through and can be seen and experienced. As we said above, we are living in this age, but getting a taste of the age to come. The ages overlap.

A final Scripture shall suffice to illustrate the overlapping nature of these last days. You know that Christ has always been God. He has always been fully God and one with the Father and the Spirit. He played a role in creation (John 1:10). He made several appearances on the earth in the Old Testament days, sometimes as the "Angel of the Lord" (Genesis 3:8, Genesis 32:25:30). King David called him Lord in his day (Psalms 110:1, Luke 20:42). And yet, despite all this, Jesus took on the role as king in a way that he had not before. Speaking of Christ, Paul says that God,

> raised him from the dead and seated him at his right hand in the heavenly realms, far above all rule and authority, power and dominion, and every title that can be given, not only in the present age but also in the one to come. And God placed all things under his feet and appointed him to be head over everything for the church, which is his body, the fullness of him who fills everything in every way (Ephesians 1:20-23).

Christ is seated on the throne with all possible power. He has all the power, rule, and authority possible *in this age and the one to come.* He has the position and authority that he has in heaven and he will have for all time. But despite all this, we do not see everyone honoring Christ and acknowledging him as God and King. He already has his authority and title, but it is not yet observed by all. How can this be? The explanation of this is, again, that we live in overlapping ages. We must continue to pray that his will be done on earth as it is in heaven (Matthew 5) precisely because it is not yet so. In this age, evil is allowed to persist. Many will not repent and confess that Jesus is lord. He is Lord–but many refuse to see it and serve him. In the age to come Christ will be acknowledged by all as Lord and Savior.

Application: The overlapping nature of these days leads to tensions. We have alluded to the tension between the new man and the old man. We have new life in Christ but continue to struggle with our old sins. We are new creatures in that we have new hearts and new desires to serve God—but we struggle with the sinful desire of the "old man," still living in our sinful flesh. We are new and old at the same time. The Holy Spirit helps us in this struggle. Those who have not tasted of the Spirit have no assistance in their fight against sin and temptations and *do not even want to join this fight.* Christians, however, have "tasted of the age to come," but we are still attracted by the temptations of this age. We are citizens of heaven and of the age to come but we live, and work, and play in this age. We have already tasted of the age to come but are not yet able to fully experience it. It is good to experience this tension. Those whose hearts are changed by God feel this struggle. Do you feel this tension in your spirit? Do you experience a closeness with God and a desire to be more with him, even as you struggle and fail in this life?

CHAPTER 5

Will there be Signs before He Returns?

Christians have debated for years whether or not there will be signs that Jesus' return is near. Some say he could return at any moment—even now—as you read this book. Others argue that the Bible teaches there are some things that must take place before Jesus returns. In this chapter we will explore what the Bible says about things that must occur before the second coming—before the glorious revealing of Jesus Christ. As we explore this question we will see that it is actually a two part question. The first part asks whether or not certain things must happen before his return. The second part, by far the more hotly debated one, asks whether or not there are *things that have yet to happen*, things for which we still wait!

Before delving into this question we must state one thing with certainty and clarity. We do not know exactly when Jesus will return and can never, under any circumstances, guess or determine the exact date until it happens. This must be the case based on what Jesus himself said about his return. He declared, "But concerning that day or that hour, no one knows, not even the angels in heaven, nor the Son, but only the Father" (Mk. 13:32). He had specifically been asked about the end of the world and his second coming. He spoke these words as a direct answer to any who might think otherwise. Unfortunately, and despite his clear warning, there have been many who have nonetheless tried to pick the date. If Jesus didn't know during his earthly ministry we ought not to think we can figure it out. With this warning in mind we can proceed cautiously to examine other things Jesus did say would have to happen before his return.

In one of his post-resurrection appearances Jesus asked Peter if Peter loved him. Peter answered that he did. Jesus responded by telling Peter to feed or take care of his sheep. In fact, Jesus asked this three times. Of course by sheep Jesus meant his people, or you might say his followers. After this touching exchange Jesus then revealed to Peter that Peter was to grow old, and that he would eventually die a horrid death.

> Truly, truly, I say to you, when you were young, you used to dress yourself and walk wherever you wanted, but when you are old, you will stretch out your hands, and another will dress you and carry you where you do not want to go. (This he said to show by what kind of death he was to glorify God.) And after saying this he said to him, "Follow me" (John 21:18-19).

Assuming Peter was approximately the same age as Jesus and old age would be considered to be at least 70 years old in time in which they lived, one would expect that Jesus' return could not be much sooner than 40 years later. By all accounts Peter is long dead! There can be no doubt that this expectation, or prophesy if you want to call it that, has been fulfilled. We no longer are waiting for this sign to occur. But remember we are dealing with a two part question—the first part asked whether or not there signs, the second part concerns whether or not all of them have been confirmed. Many people say that Jesus and the disciples did not expect signs and events before his return. It is often taught that Jesus could return at any moment. We will discuss that question later. For now it is important only to observe that this example shows there was at least one thing that had to happen before Jesus returned.

Peter's death, however, was not the only thing Jesus said would have to happen. One day upon leaving the temple Jesus became involved in a famous discussion about the temple being destroyed. Notice what Jesus says,

Jesus left the temple and was going away, when his disciples came to point out to him the buildings of the temple. But he answered them, "You see all these, do you not? Truly, I say to you, there will not be left here one stone upon another that will not be thrown down" (Matthew 24:1-2).

It is clear Jesus fully expects the temple to be destroyed before he returns. This was an unheard of concept to the Jews of the day. The temple was a magnificent structure–huge, strong, beautiful, and central to their worship and lifestyle. It was virtually inconceivable that it could be destroyed. And yet, this is exactly what Jesus had in mind. He fully expected it to be destroyed–and it would have to be destroyed in this age–before all things enter into eternity.

This temple Jesus described, the one he spoke of that day, no longer exists. As predicted, it was destroyed. History informs us that it was destroyed in 70 AD, nearly 2000 years ago. This example shows us, as did Peter dying in old age, that there were at least two things Jesus expected to happen before his return.

There is more. Jesus told Paul that he was God's chosen instrument to take the gospel to kings, to Gentiles, and all the way to Rome (see Acts 9:15, 22:21, 23:11). Paul was not even a Christian when Jesus rose from the dead and ascended into heaven. Jesus spoke to Paul from heaven after he had returned to his heavenly home. Needless to say, during his earthly ministry Jesus would not have taught that he would return at any moment. Jesus knew he would later call Paul to an international ministry. Jesus had work for Paul to do before his return. As the Bible unfolds we learn that Paul did, in fact, take the gospel to the Gentiles and even all the way to Rome. This took multiple years however. God used Paul's very imprisonment as his select means of taking the gospel to Rome. You can read this remarkable story, including Paul's incredible shipwreck and other trials, in Acts chapters 24-28. These chapters tell the exciting story of how Paul was wrongly accused and became a prisoner without a fair trial. You can read how Paul then appealed his case to Caesar–much like taking his case to the Supreme Court. As Acts chapter 28 reveals, Paul did accomplish all the things God intended concerning Rome and the Gentiles. These prophecies are fulfilled. We no longer wait for them. The point to remember however is that Jesus and the disciples would not have taught about Jesus' immediate return if there were things to be done and prophecies to be fulfilled that had to happen first. These things would take time.

Some of the things Jesus intended to be done would even take a long time. Notice what Jesus says in the parable of the nobleman going to a far country in Luke 19:11-27. The implication behind "far" country is that it will take a long time to get there and back. While gone, the man expects his servants to be doing his business "until I come." The nobleman returned after taking care of his business. This is a clear picture of Jesus leaving his people to do his bidding until he returns in his kingly role. In verse 11, when Luke introduces this parable, he informs us that the very reason Jesus told this parable was that some people *supposed* that the kingdom of God was to appear immediately. Hence Jesus is very clear that the kingdom is *not* to appear immediately–but after enough time passes for a journey to a far country. In Matthew 25:19 Jesus told a similar parable where he confirmed a delay of a long time.

We began this section with a two part question. The first part asked if there were some things that must happen before Jesus' return. We can conclude that the answer to the first question must be yes. At a minimum, Peter would get old and die, Paul would take the gospel Rome and to Gentile nations (plural!), the temple would be destroyed, and there would be a long and unspecified delay. However, it is also safe to say that all of these things have already happened. We know Paul made it to Rome, we know the temple was destroyed, we surely believe Peter has died–and I think most would agree it has been a long time–even by Biblical timelines! So can we now conclude that Jesus could return at any moment? Can we say there are no more events or prophecies that must take place first? This takes us to the second part of our question.

In answering the second question we will explore four things the Bible says will happen before Jesus returns *that have not yet happened*. These four things are in the process of happening during our day. They began to happen 2000 years ago in Jesus' day. They will continue to happen until the day Jesus returns. These things are characteristic of the time between Jesus' first and second comings. While they are in the process of happening now they will come to a climax before he returns. They must finish happening in this age–before the age to come begins. As you read on you will see what I mean. We will call these unfinished prophecies.

The first unfinished prophecy is that the gospel will be carried to all the world–specifically to all nations. This is exactly what Jesus said– "And this gospel of the kingdom will be proclaimed throughout the whole world as a testimony to all nations, and *then the end will come*" (Mt. 24:14). Jesus is very clear that the gospel will go forth as a testimony to all nations before the end. It is stated as if the going forth is in fact a condition of his return. His words concerning the woman who poured costly oil on his head confirm the same truth– "And truly, I say to you, wherever the gospel is proclaimed in the *whole world*, what she has done will be told in memory of her" (Mark 14:9, emphasis added). He simply assumes in this statement that the gospel will succeed in going to all nations.

But this is more than an assumption. It is the very heart of the work Jesus gave us to do while he is away. Recall the nobleman going on a journey to a far country? Remember they were to do his work while he was gone? We are the workers and Jesus is that Nobleman. His instructions to us, just before he left to return to heaven, concern our efforts to take the gospel to all nations. See what he says in his Great Commission to his followers,

> Go therefore and make disciples of all nations, baptizing them in the name of the Father and of the Son and of the Holy Spirit, teaching them to observe all that I have commanded you. And behold, I am with you always, to the end of the age (Matthew 28:19-20).

There has been considerable progress in taking the gospel to all nations. God is to receive glory and thanks for spreading the gospel far and wide—for making his good news available to millions of poor sinners. We ought to be especially thankful that the gospel has reached our nation—and our ears. But we also realize that the gospel has not reached all nations. God has not yet been pleased to extend his word to all peoples. But one day, the Bible tells us, this will happen. In Revelation 7:9 John sees in his vision of heaven people "from every nation, from all tribes and peoples and languages" before God's throne. We must confess that we have not been as busy as we ought to be in carrying out the Nobleman's business. And yet, we must not lose hope. In the great commission verse quoted above Jesus reminds us that we are not alone in our mission of discipling all nations. He will be with us. He will give us strength. Interestingly he also adds that he will be with us to the end of the age. He will be with us through his Holy Spirit. Recall our previous discussion about this age and the age to come? We noted that his coming marks the end of this age and the beginning of the age to come—the eternal age. He will assist us in our task of taking the gospel to all nations; the completion of this task, along with the others described below, will mark the end of the age. "And this gospel of the kingdom will be proclaimed throughout the whole world as a testimony to all nations, and *then the end will come.*" The world will receive a testimony before Jesus returns.

The second unfinished prophecy we will discuss is the revealing of the Antichrist—the lawless one, sometimes called the son of perdition. We know that this person will become public before the end because the apostle Paul tells us so. Read his words:

> Let no one deceive you in any way. For that day will not come, unless the rebellion comes first, and the man of lawlessness is revealed, the son of destruction, who opposes and exalts himself against every so-called god or object of worship, so that he takes his seat in the temple of God, proclaiming himself to be God. Do you not remember that when I was still with you I told you these things? And you know what is restraining him now so that he may be revealed in his time. For the mystery of lawlessness is already at work. Only he who now restrains it will do so until he is out of the

way. And then the lawless one will be revealed, whom the Lord Jesus will kill with the breath of his mouth and bring to nothing by the appearance of his coming. The coming of the lawless one is by the activity of Satan with all power and false signs and wonders (2 Thessalonians 2:3-9).

Paul is teaching about the day of the Lord, the day Jesus returns. Note that he says the day will not come *unless* the "man of lawlessness" is revealed. This "son of perdition" sets himself up against God–his working is according to the power of Satan. Do you know who this person is? Can anyone name him? It is clear that this person has not yet been identified. At present he is being restrained–but he has already begun his work. His evil work will increase to the point that Jesus himself will need to come and "kill him with the breath of his mouth."

John also makes a reference to the coming of the antichrist. John indicates that the antichrist is coming and yet also says many antichrists have already come (1 Jn. 2:18). Remember what was said about the prophecies that are in the process of happening now but will come to a climax before he returns? They must finish happening in this age–before the age to come begins. This is one of those things. Many antichrists–that is–those acting in the interest of Satan–are already active in the world. Anyone who opposes God and his people is an antichrist to some extent. But John indicates that *the* antichrist is yet to come.

The third unfinished prophecy is tribulation. Tribulation involves persecution, trials, and painful experiences. The Bible teaches that God's people will experience intense tribulation before Jesus returns. Just as with the spreading of the gospel and the little antichrists, tribulation is already occurring but will increase and reach a climax before the return of the Lord Jesus. In his famous sermon on the Mount of Olives Jesus said to his disciples "Then they will deliver you up to tribulation and put you to death, and you will be hated by all nations for my name's sake" (Matthew 24:9). Notice that he uses the phrase "all nations" as he did when he spoke of the gospel going to "all nations." It is likely that these two things go hand-in-hand. As the gospel goes forth to all nations some people will receive it with joy–others, including the little antichrists, will turn and persecute disciples. The persecutions will increase and intensify until the final antichrist appears and requires Jesus himself to appear and save his people.

Jesus was very clear about the order of events concerning the climax of the tribulation and his return:

> Immediately after the tribulation of those days the sun will be darkened, and the moon will not give its light, and the stars will fall from heaven, and the powers of the heavens will be shaken. Then will appear in heaven the sign of the Son of Man, and then all the tribes of the earth will mourn, and they will see the Son of Man coming on the clouds of heaven with power and great glory (Matthew 24:29-30).

We should expect tribulation in our lives. We should expect it as we take the gospel to new lands. We should expect it to increase as we get closer and closer to Jesus' return–to increase to the point that it would appear to be unbearable. We should remember to pray for Christians in places (like China) where persecution of Christians is already much worse than it is here at home.

The fourth and final unfinished prophecy we will consider is the "rebellion," also referred to as the "falling away" or the "apostasy." When Christians use the word apostasy we mean a turning away from the truth. Some who profess to follow Christ will actually prove to be false disciples–not disciples at all! They will fall away, or turn away from the truth, and from following Christ. This falling away will take place before the day of the Lord's return. See how Paul describes it.

> Let no one deceive you by any means; for that day will not come unless the *rebellion* comes first, and the man of sin is revealed, the son of perdition, who opposes and exalts himself above all that is called God or that is worshipped, so that he sits as God in the temple of God, showing himself that he is God (2 Thessalonians 2:3-4).

Like the other unfinished prophecies this one is already happening. However, also like the others, this one will intensify until it reaches a climax. Paul refers to *the* falling away and it is connected to the working of the antichrist–the man of sin we discussed earlier.

All four of the expected events are related. The gospel goes forth to the whole world. As it does, persecution increases. The personal antichrist drives this persecution and finally appears on the scene himself. As a result of the persecution many will fall away. As these things unfold and intensify the gospel reaches all the intended recipients. Those who will fall away do so. The antichrist is revealed. Persecution rises to the point even true Christians may have trouble withstanding it. Then, when these things have happened, we can expect the Lord to appear.

Application: It is well worth noting that these last four things, the things that have not been completed, are underway in our day. The gospel is spreading to the entire world. Many antichrists have *already* appeared. Many Christians *already* experience tribulation. Many false but professing believers have *already* fallen away. These things are already happening–but they are not complete. There will be intensification, and a climax. The gospel will reach the whole world. *The* antichrist will appear. We will suffer *the* tribulation. We will sadly see *the* falling away. We do not know when these things will be. We do not even know exactly what reaching the whole world with the gospel will look like. Surely it does not mean every single person becomes a Christian. But on the other hand, we can expect that every people group hears a credible presentation of the gospel, sufficient that some from each tribe and tongue call upon the name of the Lord. We will see them in heaven (Rev. 5:9). This uncertainty keeps us from predicting the time of the Lord's return. He cautioned us many times while on earth the first time to be ready–for we do not know when the Master comes. This uncertainty should serve to keep us on our guard. We must take care that we do not fall away. We must do our part to take the gospel to the world. We must ask ourselves how we will stand in the face of persecution.

CHAPTER 6

Can we Determine the Order of Future Events?

In this chapter we will attempt to determine the order in which we expect future events to occur. Notice we are concerned with the *order*—we are certainly not trying to guess or determine the *date*. Recall Jesus himself did not even have this information when he was on earth. In previous chapters we have already spoken of the resurrection, the last day, the judgment, and eternity. In this chapter we will introduce some additional topics and attempt to get them in the right chronological order.

To begin, it will be helpful to return to an important clue from the Book of John that we previously discussed. You may remember that John said the resurrection would take place on the last day. He also said the judgment would take place on the last day. We drew the obvious conclusion that the resurrection and judgment occur on the same day, the last one. This is not all, however, that we can conclude from these facts. These two events, the resurrection and the judgment, surely occur in a particular order. It is not logical to think that the judgment should come before the resurrection. Surely it is more likely God will resurrect men *before* he judges them. This is in fact what we find in many Scriptures. Notice what is implied in Paul's statement to the Corinthians, "For we must all appear before the judgment seat of Christ, so that each one may receive what is due for what he has done in the body, whether good or evil" (2 Corinthians 5:10). Those who have died must *appear*. It is reasonable to conclude they will first be resurrected. His words to the Romans are more direct,

Why do you pass judgment on your brother? Or you, why do you despise your brother? For we will all stand before the judgment seat of God; for it is written, "As I live, says the Lord, every knee shall bow to me, and every tongue shall confess to God" (Romans 14:10-11).

Standing, bowing, and confessing certainly seem to indicate bodies will be present. If all are to do this, those who have died must first be resurrected.

Having concluded that the resurrection occurs before the judgment we can now examine other closely related events. One of the most valuable passages in this respect is First Thessalonians 4:13-5:11. We will not quote this long passage here but recommend that you read it two or three times before continuing.

Paul is writing to comfort grieving Corinthians concerning their Christian loved ones and friends who have died. In doing so, he gives us valuable information about the order of future events. First, he notes that God will bring the dead with him when he comes. He evidently means their souls, or spirits, since their bodies will be in graves or elsewhere on the earth. The living will not precede or gain any advantage over those who have died (v. 14-15). The dead have not lost their place in line, so to speak, to the living. The dead are actually moved to the front of the line by having died! When the Lord descends from heaven the dead (their bodies) will rise first (v. 15). Their bodies will be reunited with their spirits. Then, following the rising of the dead, the living will be caught up with the resurrected dead (v. 17) to meet the Lord in the air and be with him forever. The phrase "caught up" has given rise to the word "rapture," popular in modern discussions about Christ's return. We will discuss the rapture later. Paul then underscores part of his reason for writing in verse 18–"comfort one another with these words." But he doesn't leave them with only this command to be comforted. He reminds them that the Day of the Lord will come as a thief in the night–at an unknown time and season (5:1-2). They are warned to be sober-minded, to be ready (5:6). The reason is clear in verse 9–his coming means salvation for some, but wrath for others–the two and only two outcomes of the judgment.

We can summarize the order in First Thessalonians as follows: 1) The Lord comes with the souls of those who have died. 2) The bodies of the dead rise. 3) The living rise (including those formerly dead). 4) The righteous meet the Lord in the air. 5) They live with Christ forever. We've already concluded above from John 6:39-40 that the resurrection is on the last day. Thus, since the resurrection accompanies his return and our being caught up to meet him, they must also be on the last day–the Day of the Lord. We see this day is appropriately named–*he* descends, the living and the resurrected saints rise to meet *him* in the air, and *he* presides over the judgment. It is *his* day.

Evidently the Thessalonians had recurring problems or questions concerning the return of Christ. While it would be appropriate to sympathize with their concerns, their problems have proven to be to our advantage. Paul would not have written these things (which benefit us) had they not had these struggles. In his second letter to the Thessalonians Paul reinforces what he said in his first letter. Read carefully Second Thessalonians 1:4-10 and 2:1-3:

> Therefore we ourselves boast about you in the churches of God for your steadfastness and faith in all your persecutions and in the afflictions that you are enduring. This is evidence of the righteous *judgment* of God, that you may be considered worthy of the kingdom of God, for which you are also *suffering*–since indeed God considers it just to repay with affliction those who afflict you, and to *grant relief* to you who are *afflicted* as well as to us, *when the Lord Jesus is revealed from heaven* with his mighty angels in flaming fire, *inflicting vengeance* on those who do not know God and on those who do not obey the gospel of our Lord Jesus. They will suffer the punishment of *eternal destruction*, away from the presence of the Lord and from the glory of his might, *when he comes on that day* to be glorified in his saints, and to be marveled at among all who have believed, because our testimony to you was believed.
>
> Now concerning the *coming* of our Lord Jesus Christ and our being *gathered* together to him, we ask you, brothers, not to be quickly shaken in mind or alarmed, either by a spirit or a spoken word, or a letter seeming to be from us, to the effect that the day of the Lord has come. Let no one deceive you in any way. *For that day will not*

come, unless the rebellion comes first, and the *man of lawlessness is revealed,* the son of destruction (emphasis added).

Paul notes that the Lord comes to take vengeance on those who persecute his saints (v. 6). He punishes our enemies and at the same time grants us relief. We see that these two things often go together in the Bible. He does this when he is "revealed" (v. 7) on that day (v. 10). The only possible day Paul could mean is the Day of the Lord–the day he previously wrote them about. The wicked then receive "eternal destruction" (v. 9). This is obviously the same judgment he referenced in First Thessalonians. The point is that the saints suffer up until the Day he returns to execute final judgment. We should not expect relief before then. We are to persevere. Interestingly, Paul then joins the Lord's coming and our gathering together with him as one big event in the first verse of chapter 2. This coming and gathering occur on "that day" (v. 3). He then reminds his readers that that day will not come unless the apostasy comes first and the Son of Perdition is revealed. All these events occur on that day, the Day of the Lord–just as the Old Testament prophets foretold. There are not multiple days, multiple comings, multiple judgments. There is a day he returns. The order of events can be depicted as follows:

**Coming → dead rise → living rise → meet in the air →
Christ judges → eternity begins.**

It really is that simple. This does not mean we have (or will!) answer all questions. It does mean however, that the Bible makes it very simple to discern the basic order of the main events we expect to happen on the last day. To sum up what we have said so far, recall that during these last days we see professing Christians falling away, we see tribulation (persecution), we see many little antichrists, and we see the gospel going to all the world. These are things we see in the last days (plural). The coming, rising, meeting in the air and judgment are what we expect on the last day (singular). The next 4 chapters will discuss these events in the order in which we expect them to occur.

Application: Paul was clear that when Jesus returns he will inflict vengeance on those who persecute his followers. There are those who persecute–and there are those who are persecuted. Those who follow Christ in this age should expect persecution. We should expect to suffer *because* we are Christians. We will have relief when he returns. Our enemies will suffer vengeance. Are you a follower of Christ or are you a persecutor? You can either expect relief when he comes or you can expect the punishment of eternal destruction. You are either for him or you are against him (Matthew 12:30). There is no other option.

CHAPTER 7

The Resurrection

The belief in the bodily resurrection is a basic tenet or doctrine of Christianity. One could scarcely claim to be a Christian if he denied the resurrection of Christ. Only a young or uninformed Christian would be unaware of the expected resurrection of every person—believers and non-believers. Jesus himself said this is the expectation of those who believe in him, that they should have eternal life and that he would raise them up at the last day. Martha had this expectation for Lazarus—"I know he will rise again in the resurrection on the last day" (John 11:24). This chapter will look at what the Bible teaches about the resurrection. In the last chapter we established the order of events that take place on the last day. Recall we said they were his coming—the dead rising—the living rising to meet him in the air—Christ judging—and all people entering eternity. We have already discussed the fact of Christ's return in the first chapter. There we discussed the three main words used to describe his coming. They were the words "coming," "revealing," and "appearing." Here we turn to the second great event on that great day—the resurrection.

There are many striking features concerning the resurrection of our bodies from the dust of the earth. We shall focus on two in this chapter. First, we shall confirm that there is one future and lasting resurrection of all men who have ever died. Second, we will look at the bodies that result from this resurrection.

There is *one* future and lasting resurrection with a couple of exceptions. We must begin our study of this first point by explaining why we say future and lasting and why we make a couple of exceptions. When we have discussed the resurrection so far, we have meant the resurrection that is yet to occur in the future. It will be the final one; it will be the one that lasts. Obviously there have been numerous resurrections in the past. You might recall Lazarus, or perhaps the widow's son raised from the dead by Elijah. These were certainly real resurrections. They were not, however, the final resurrection. Lazarus, the widow's son, and all other resurrections that occurred so far were temporary–these people had the unusual experience of dying again! Their resurrection did not last. These resurrections were performed to prove some point or establish some fact in the immediate present. For example, Lazarus's resurrection served to establish the fact that Jesus had the power over death and that he was (and is) God. Elijah was given power to prove his credentials as a true prophet of the living God. However, we know these are not to be confused with *the* resurrection of the last day. Recall the order of events that we discussed in the last chapter. Following the resurrection there is the judgment that leads to either heaven or hell. Lazarus and the widow's son were resurrected, got up, walked around, and proceeded to lead an otherwise normal life–they did *not* face judgment and did not at that time enter heaven or hell. Therefore, these resurrections cannot be the final resurrection–we expect the future resurrection to be final and lead to eternity.

We must also make an exception of Christ when discussing the future and final resurrection because he has already experienced his final resurrection. He did not and will not die again. His resurrection is lasting. Furthermore, he has entered heaven, even heaven itself as Hebrews says (9:4). Finally, unlike Lazarus and the widow's son, Jesus has received his new body, which we will discuss below. Therefore, we must say that everyone who has died or ever will die, except Christ, is still waiting for their future and lasting resurrection.

When we said there is one future and lasting resurrection we specifically meant *one*. There is to be *one* resurrection that covers Christians and non-Christians alike. While most passages focus on Christians and the benefits to be found in Christ, there are passages which address the wicked as well. We will now look at some of the Biblical evidence that confirms our conclusion that there is one resurrection and that it is final, lasting, and leads to either heaven or hell.

Jesus describes this future event in the following way:

> For as the Father has life in himself, so he has granted the Son also to have life in himself. And he has given him authority to execute judgment, because he is the Son of Man. Do not marvel at this, for an hour is coming when all who are in the tombs will hear his voice and come out, those who have done good to the resurrection of life, and those who have done evil to the resurrection of judgment (John 5:26-29).

Jesus says all who are in the tombs will hear his voice and come out. Notice that some will face a resurrection of life and others a resurrection of judgment. They are not resurrected like Lazarus–who rose and resumed living as he had lived before he died. Jesus specifically mentions that an hour is coming–there is an appointed time in the future when the resurrection will occur and people will face judgment. Christians will enter eternal life. Non-Christians will enter eternal torment in hell.

Thousands of years before, Daniel describes this aspect of the Day of the Lord in similar terms:

> At that time shall arise Michael, the great prince who has charge of your people. And there shall be a time of trouble, such as never has been since there was a nation till that time. But at that time your people shall be delivered, everyone whose name shall be found written in the book. And many of those who sleep in the dust of the earth shall awake, some to everlasting life, and some to shame and everlasting contempt (Daniel 12:1-2).

Daniel speaks of a time in the future. He speaks of those who sleep in the dust of the earth, meaning those who have died. And he speaks of some entering eternal life and of others entering eternal contempt–you might say punishment. They do not get up and resume normal life–they enter eternity. They do not die another physical death. There is a time when this happens. This is important to note–Daniel does not say times, plural, just as Jesus said hour and not hours. There is not one time for the Christians and one time for the wicked but "a time" and "an hour" when the righteous and wicked both rise. This again confirms what we have said about there being one, future, and lasting resurrection.

One final passage from Paul will be helpful to underscore this point. He said:

> I worship the God of our fathers, believing everything laid down by the Law and written in the Prophets, having a hope in God, which these men themselves accept, that there will be a resurrection of both the just and the unjust (Acts 24:14b-15).

Note that Paul also refers to a single resurrection—one resurrection of both the just and the unjust. By just and unjust he means the righteous, or Christians, and the wicked, or non-Christians. He also refers to the resurrection as still future when he says "there will be" a resurrection.

Our second objective was to look at the bodies that will result from this one, future, and lasting resurrection. From what has been discussed above you may have already concluded that the resurrection will result in a physical body. You may have thought about Christ's resurrection resulting in a physical body. I hope you made this conclusion! Too many people today have false impressions of heaven and of the resurrection. The popular conception of heaven seems to involve spirits floating in the clouds singing and playing harps all day! Where do people get such notions? Not from the Bible to be sure! These ideas come from television, from advertisements, and from misleading children's stories. Be careful where you get your information about God—it is a life and death matter. Jesus was clear about his resurrection body. There is no way to miss this in what he said to his disciples after he rose from the grave.

> "See my hands and my feet, that it is I myself. Touch me, and see. For a spirit does not have flesh and bones as you see that I have." And when he had said this, he showed them his hands and his feet. And while they still disbelieved for joy and were marveling, he said

to them, "Have you anything here to eat?" They gave him a piece of broiled fish, and he took it and ate before them (Luke 24:39-43).

Notice all the clear indications of a body. Jesus emphatically indicates he has hands and feet. He encourages them to touch him–something you cannot do to a spirit. This is, in fact, the very thing that differentiates between a spirit and a physical being. But this is not all–Jesus wanted to feed his body. They gave him some fish and he ate it. His body was very clearly real.

Jesus gave a second confirmation that his resurrected body was real. He encouraged Thomas to place his hand in his (Jesus' side) and feel where the Roman soldier had pierced him with his spear (John 20:27). Again, the hole and scar would not be present in a spirit, only in a real physical body.

You may have also suspected that the resurrection involved a body based on the Daniel passage quoted above about those sleeping in the dust waking to life or to judgment. While the concept of waking may not prove beyond doubt that the resurrection is physical it does imply it. However, there are a couple Old Testament passages that would appear to prove convincingly that Old Testament believers were well aware of the bodily resurrection. Note what Isaiah said in chapter 26 verse 19, "Your dead shall live; their bodies shall rise. You who dwell in the dust, awake and sing for joy! For your dew is a dew of light, and the earth will give birth to the dead."

He clearly says their bodies shall rise. Isaiah allows for no lonesome spirits floating in the clouds!

Job, even earlier than Isaiah, taught the same thing:

For I know that my Redeemer lives, and at the last he will stand upon the earth. And after my skin has been thus destroyed, yet in my flesh I shall see God, whom I shall see for myself, and my eyes shall behold, and not another. My heart faints within me! (Job 19:25-27)

Job expected that long after he had died and his body had decayed ("after my skin has been thus destroyed") that in his resurrected

Job expected that long after he had died and his body had decayed ("after my skin has been thus destroyed") that in his resurrected new body he would see God. He would be *back* in his flesh–resurrected in a fleshly body–and he would stand in the presence of God. This was Job's hope. It can be ours as well. Paul said that those who belong to Christ will receive life in their "mortal bodies" from the Holy Spirit (Romans 8:11).

Having established that the resurrected body will be physical we spend a little time examining the qualities of this body. We shall make a brief investigation into the nature of the body we expect to receive in the future resurrection. It will be a physical body but it will be special and different in a number of ways from our current bodies. We have drawn the conclusion that the resurrected body is physical because Jesus' body was physical. Is this a fair conclusion? I would like to answer that it is. In fact, we are invited to make a comparison of our resurrected body with Jesus'. John tells us that even though what we will be has not been fully revealed we do know that when he returns we will be like him (1 John 3:2)! Despite the fact that this seems too good to be true, God's children shall actually be made like Christ!

Jesus' resurrected body was in some ways like his body that died. For instance, it must have looked somewhat the same for most people recognized him immediately (although the disciples on the road to Emmaus seemed to have difficulty in doing so). Also, his resurrected body was able to eat. However, it was evidently different in some ways as well. Notice that he was apparently able to pass through solid walls or doors with his new body:

> Eight days later, his disciples were inside again, and Thomas was with them. Although the doors were locked, Jesus came and stood among them and said, "Peace be with you" (John 20:19).

The doors were locked. He somehow appeared in the room.

Jesus evidently had the ability, in his resurrected body, to ascend to the Father and then return to earth. Mary (who also did not

Do not cling to me, for I have not yet ascended to the Father; but go to my brothers and say to them, "I am ascending to my Father and your Father, to my God and your God" (John 20:17).

He had to ascend. Of course, he later appeared on earth for another 40 days.

Application: We cannot say that our resurrected bodies will be exactly like Jesus'. We will not have his scars. We do know however, that when he returns we will be like him (1 John 6:32). This is a staggering thought. We will be like Jesus. Our bodies will be significantly changed. They will not be exactly like they are now, but will be like his glorious body (Philippians 3:20-21). We were created to bear his image. We do this poorly now. We will do so much better then.

CHAPTER 8

The New Body

In the last chapter we established the fact that in the resurrection Christians will rise with new bodies. They will be like Jesus' body. His body was physical. His body took up space. His body could be touched. It could eat. These are all things we infer by looking at Jesus' body and assuming ours will be similar. These are reasonable assumptions. However, what *can* we say with certainty that the Bible teaches about the resurrected body?

The apostle Paul gives us some additional information about our new bodies in First Corinthians chapter 15. He does this by way of an extended analogy. He compares a dying and resurrected body to a seed that falls to the ground and dies, only to "rise" to life in a new form. Notice that the nature of the new body is the specific question Paul is addressing, "But someone will ask, "How are the dead raised? With what kind of body do they come?" (v. 35). Paul has much to say about the new body. He draws numerous comparisons in this passage. We will only look at three, however. They are summarized in verses 42 and 43. These verses are printed below. It will be helpful if you read the entire passage from verse 35 through the end of the chapter.

> So is it with the resurrection of the dead. What is sown is perishable; what is raised is imperishable. It is sown in dishonor; it is raised in glory. It is sown in weakness; it is raised in power (1 Corinthians 15:42-43).

First, Paul notes that when a seed is planted in the ground it dies (v. 36). It dies in the sense that the seed breaks down in the presence of soil, moisture, and sunlight and it ceases to exist as a seed. It can be said to have died or to have perished. It only lives a short time as a seed–only a few months or perhaps a couple seasons–from the time seeds fall in autumn until they sprout in the spring. But it rises from the ground with new life. It is no longer a seed–it is a tree or some other plant. Paul argues that the relationship between our current body and our new body is like the relationship between the seed and the tree. The old body, like the seed, dies and is buried in the ground. The new body, like the new plant, rise from the ground changed, even new and improved.

Adam and Eve were created with bodies that had no flaws. They had not been marred by sin, like all mankind since then except Christ. Once they sinned however, their bodies began to die. They began to get sick, to experience pain and suffer injuries. All of our bodies are beginning to die before they are even born. The impacts of sin begin causing us problems while we are yet in our mother's womb. But when we receive our heavenly bodies they will be imperishable. They cannot die nor can they suffer any of the consequences of sin that lead to death. The new bodies won't get sick. They won't break. They won't wear out. This of course becomes more and more meaningful to a person the older he gets! Most children think their bodies are just fine–they can run, jump, play and never seem to get tired. They rarely get sore and stiff the next morning. Their joints don't ache after moderate exercise. But the older we get, and you could think of your parents or grandparents (or the author of this book!), the more we appreciate the hope of a new body.

Of course, the good things we are discussing about the new body pertain to those who are Christians. We will have a body perfectly suited for life in the new world–in heaven with Christ. Those who are not followers of Christ, those whose sins are not forgiven, they too will receive new bodies–only they will not be suited for heaven–they will be suited to an eternity of suffering. Instead of being resurrected to life, they will experience a resurrection to death.

Second, Paul notes that our bodies are sown in dishonor but are raised in glory (by sown he means they are buried). A seed is usually not much to look at but it produces a beautiful plant.

Similarly, our bodies die and go into the ground in dishonor but rise in glory. To bury a body is an unnatural thing. We were created to live–and had Adam not sinned he would have lived forever. Death is, in a real sense, a very unnatural and dishonorable thing. There is nothing honorable about a body that has no life. It does not serve well in its role as a bearer of God's image. Despite the best efforts of those who officiate at funerals this will be the case. This is not to say the person is not "honored" by the words spoken about them or people's memories of them. Fallen soldiers are given full military honors when they are buried. But what Paul is saying is that a dead body is not an honorable thing–it was designed by God to be alive–to live–and now it is not doing that. Man was given the charge of subduing the earth (Genesis 1:28)–to farm it and use it for his needs. In death, man is placed inside the earth and the earth subdues him. This is a reversal of the created order–things are turned upside down. This is dishonorable.

When the Christian's body is raised, it is no longer in a dishonorable state–it is raised in glory. This means the new body will posses dignity, honor, and majesty. This word *glory* is the same word used to describe Christ himself when he returns at his second coming. It is a remarkable concept that resurrected Christians will share some of the same characteristics of Christ himself–but this is exactly what Paul is saying. Our new bodies will be glorious.

Third, Paul says the body, again like the seed, is sown in weakness but raised in power. While Paul does not give details about the power we are raised with, we do know something about what weak means. A dead body has no strength. It can do nothing. There is a sense in which this is true of a seed. It does nothing on its own. It relies on forces outside itself to make it sprout and grow. It relies on heat from the sun and on moisture from the ground. The body, sown in weakness, can do nothing on its own to bring it back to life, to bring about its own resurrection. It is altogether dependant on an outside force.

Interestingly, all these changes are necessary in order for us to enter heaven. We cannot enter heaven as we are. Our natural, made-from-dust perishable bodies *cannot* inherit the kingdom of

God! Paul says it simply cannot be done (v. 50). He does not give a detailed explanation but does point out that the perishable cannot inherit the imperishable. Our present bodies are not worthy to partake of the pleasures of heaven and of God's presence–nor would they be able to enjoy it fully. We must be changed; we must be made glorious; our bodies must be made strong; we must be changed from a "natural" state into a "spiritual" state (v. 44). All these things God does for us. "But thanks be to God, who gives us the victory through our Lord Jesus Christ" (v. 57).

Throughout this whole discussion we have talked all around an important point without ever actually mentioning it. We have spoken of our body being changed; of our body dying and being raised; of taking on strength and glory. We have spoken of a new body–and a new body it is. But it is not entirely new. In some ways it is still the old body, but the old body repaired, radically new and improved. There is *continuity* between the old and new bodies–the person inside the body continues to be the same person. Paul spoke as if he fully expected himself to be included in the resurrection, not swapped; he would not cease to exist and be replaced by an entirely new person named Paul. He spoke of himself ("we") being *changed.* He himself would survive death and burial. Paul expected to die and Paul expected to live again–it was Paul who would die and be placed into the grave and the same Paul would rise from the grave alive. Jesus died and was buried. The same Jesus rose again. The gospel would be meaningless if it were otherwise as Christ would not have actually conquered death. He would not have removed the sting and power of death. Job had the same expectation, that after *he* died *he* would again see God (19:25). There was continuity for Job, for Jesus, and for Paul and Paul's readers, and there will be continuity for all Christians who die.

This is also clear from Paul's seed analogy. While the seed dies, the plant that comes from the ground is the same biological life that was in the seed. The seed and the tree are linked. The seed was not completely destroyed; the seed was turned into the tree, so to speak. The seed no longer existed *as a seed*, but it continued to exist *as a tree*. In our resurrection we will still be people, men and women–our external form will not be changed in the way a seed

CHAPTER 8 – *The New Body*

becomes a tree. However, our natures will become better in ways far more glorious, far more powerful, and far more imperishable. We do not cease to exist, rather we *put on* the imperishable and we *put on* immortality.

The concept of the resurrection is difficult for many to believe. There may be many reasons for this. We are often told by skeptics that miracles do not occur. We are not accustomed to witnessing resurrections. It may seem to many to be too good to be true. But the Bible gives us hope and assurance that those who follow Christ will be resurrected. As we close this chapter we shall look at the reason we are *assured* that the resurrection will happen. That reason, in one word, is Christ.

Jesus had been teaching the disciples in the upper room shortly before his betrayal and death. They had expressed some fears about being left alone and Jesus was reassuring them. In the midst of this discussion Jesus explained to Phillip that though the world would see him no more, Phillip would see him again. Then Jesus made what is a most reassuring statement, "Because I live you will live also" (John 14:19). Jesus' point was that because he, Jesus, would live again, Phillip would also live again. Jesus' resurrection was the guarantee of our resurrection. You are familiar with the concept of a guarantee. When someone is buying a house or other very expensive item they are required to make a large payment up front as a promise that they will pay the rest later. The money paid up front is a guarantee of later payments. In the same way, Jesus' resurrection was the promise that others would be raised later.

Paul taught this same concept just before he introduced the seed analogy we discussed above. Using another agricultural metaphor, he explained that Christ was the *first-fruits* and that the rest of us would be raised at his coming (1 Corinthians 15:20, 23). Here Paul uses an illustration from the Old Testament that modern readers may not be familiar with. The Jews celebrated a festival called First-fruits in which they celebrated the harvest of some of the earliest fruits and produce their farms yielded for the year. These were their first-fruits and they made offerings of them unto the Lord. They understood that because the ground had produced these early first fruits and vegetables it was a sure thing that the ground would later yield the full crop. The first-fruits were the promise, or guarantee, of the full harvest. Paul then uses this imagery to illustrate that Christ's resurrection is the first-fruit that assures the full resurrection of his people when he returns.

In closing we will say a word about when this resurrection will occur. John records an important discussion between Jesus and Martha following Lazarus's death. Their loved one had died and Mary and Martha were understandably upset. Adding pain to the loss of their loved one, they believed that had Jesus hurried to their home he could have saved Lazarus's life. Jesus however, had tarried a bit so that he could raise Lazarus from the dead and thereby display his power and give glory to God. It was a "greater miracle," so to speak, to raise him than to merely make him well. Jesus spoke to Martha, intending to comfort her, with these words, "Your brother will rise again" (John 11:23). Notice Martha's informative response in the next verse, "I know that he will rise again in the resurrection on the last day." Martha already knew her brother would rise and that he would rise on the last day! This is telling. She knew this either from reading the Old Testament or from other things Jesus had recently taught. The New Testament had not been written at this time. Paul, who wrote much about the resurrection and the last day, was not even a Christian at this point. The resurrection was a basic fact understood by Martha. She was no prophecy expert, not a scholar, not a priest, a scribe, or a Levite. She simply had an understanding and a firm faith that there would be a resurrection on the last day.

Application: Christ is the first-fruits of a great harvest. He came, lived, and died with a purpose. He intends to secure many people to worship him and to enjoy his presence forever. God has promised that if his Holy Spirit lives in you, he will raise you from the dead just as he raised Christ (Romans 8:11). We have the guarantee of Christ's resurrection *and* the promise of God: God's Word and his deed. God also intends that Christ is to be the firstborn among many brothers (Romans 8:29). Are you one of them?

CHAPTER 9

Meeting Christ in the Air

We closed chapter six with the following order of events that occur along with and as a part of the second coming:

Coming → dead rise → living rise → meet in the air → Christ judges → eternity begins.

We have discussed the coming of Christ. We have noted that he is revealed and that he is said to "appear." We have just finished discussing the resurrection and the new body. We observed how the Bible teaches that the dead will be resurrected. They will be wondrously brought back to life. In this chapter we will look further at what happens to the dead when they rise. We will look specifically at what is involved in meeting Christ in the air. Our key passage is First Thessalonians 4:13-18:

> But we do not want you to be uninformed, brothers, about those who are asleep, that you may not grieve as others do who have no hope. For since we believe that Jesus died and rose again, even so, through Jesus, God will bring with him those who have fallen asleep. For this we declare to you by a word from the Lord, that we who are alive, who are left until the coming of the Lord, will not precede those who have fallen asleep. For the Lord himself will descend from heaven with a cry of command, with the voice of an archangel, and with the sound of the trumpet of God. And the dead in Christ will rise first. Then we who are alive, who are left, will be caught up together with them in the clouds to meet the Lord in the air, and so we will always be with the Lord. Therefore encourage one another with these words.

In this passage Paul's main purpose in writing is to comfort Thessalonian Christians who had lost loved ones due to death. Paul says they ought not grieve as unbelievers do, since they would see these loved ones again. Paul makes the incredible statement that when Christ returns he will bring with him those Christians who had died! This must have been an amazing comfort to them as it ought to be to us. Our friends and family members who died "in the Lord," that is, those who were Christians, will return with the Lord when he comes again. Though his main purpose is to encourage these concerned believers, Paul writes much that helps us understand how events on the last day will unfold. We will need to examine the many parts of this passage in detail.

He begins his argument with the statement that "since we believe that Jesus died and rose again." This is foundational. Paul is writing to people who have this belief. The comfort he describes in Christ is available to those who believe Jesus died and rose again. Those who do not believe this, Paul refers to as those who have "no hope." What a depressing condition it would be to have no hope. Since Paul's readers believe the truth about the resurrection, they also can believe Jesus will bring the Christian dead with him when he returns from heaven and that he will resurrect their bodies as well. Recall what we said in the last chapter about Christ being the first-fruits of the harvest (1 Corinthians 15:20-23). The rest of the harvest will be brought and resurrected at his coming. These two passages refer to the same event—Christ's coming.

Paul teaches an amazing series of events. First, Christ brings with him those Christians who have died. Second, the bodies of dead Christians rise from the earth. Third, those who just rose from the dead along with those who had not died will rise to meet the Lord in the air. Fourth, this group will always be with the Lord. Paul then instructs us to comfort one another with these words. We shall examine each of these steps in this chapter.

Have you considered what is implied by Christ bringing Christians with him when he comes? Have you wondered where the dead Christians go after they die? Have you wondered what it is like after death? These are things you must think about someday. And now is a good time to think about them. When we read that Christ will be bringing people with him when he comes, it makes us think these people must be with him now! And that is exactly what the Bible teaches. When Christians die, their soul goes to be with Christ. Only their body stays behind and is placed in a grave. Death itself may be unpleasant, but the time after death is a time for the Christian to joyfully anticipate. Notice how Paul anticipated the time in Philippians 1:21-23:

> For to me to live is Christ, and to die is gain. If I am to live in the flesh, that means fruitful labor for me. Yet which I shall choose I cannot tell. I am hard pressed between the two. My desire is to depart and be with Christ, for that is far better.

Paul's *desire* is to depart and be with Christ. That is better! Interestingly, Paul does not desire to be in heaven; he desires to be with Christ. This is an important distinction. Paul is not so excited about being in a *place* when he dies. Rather, he desires to be with a *Person*. We shall look at this issue in more detail in a latter chapter. For now we shall note only that the spirits of these Christian dead are with Christ and will be with him when he returns to the earth. This should comfort and encourage us, as Paul commands.

You may be wondering if there is a connection between the spirits returning with Christ and the bodies rising from the grave. There is indeed a connection! These spirits will be united with their perfected bodies that have just risen from the grave. The spirits of the dead Christians have been with Christ. However, despite being with Christ, they are somehow incomplete! This is amazing, but true. God created man as a spiritual being–but also as a being with a body. Our body is part of the physical creation that God declared good, even very good (Genesis 1:31). God's original creation was designed not for spirits alone, but for men with bodies. The body continues to be important to God.

Similarly, when Christ came to earth he did so by taking on flesh–a normal, mortal human body. When he died, his spirit departed but his body remained and was placed in a tomb. Notice that Jesus himself confirms this about his own Spirit, "Then Jesus, calling out with a loud voice, said, "Father, into your hands I commit my spirit!" And having said this he breathed his last (Luke 23:46). His Spirit was in the hands of the Father while his body was in the grave. But three days later Jesus' body was made alive–it was resurrected–and it was resurrected as a perfect body. Furthermore, it was reunited with his spirit. There was no stranger inhabiting Jesus' body–it was his body and it was his spirit. It was the spirit Jesus had three days earlier given into the Father's hand and the same body that had been placed in the tomb.

Likewise, when the spirits of believers return with Christ at his second coming, they too shall be united with their newly resurrected bodies. These too will be changed bodies, perfect bodies, as Paul states,

> Behold! I tell you a mystery. We shall not all sleep, but we shall all be changed, in a moment, in the twinkling of an eye, at the last trumpet. For the trumpet will sound, and the dead will be raised imperishable, and we shall be changed. For this perishable body must put on the imperishable, and this mortal body must put on immortality (1 Corinthians 15:52-53).

The dead will be raised imperishable. This means they can never perish, or die again. This should give great comfort to those of us who have lost Christian loved ones and friends. We should eagerly await this day. But there is more! Paul expects the living to be changed as well. Notice in the passage he is referring to the living as those who "shall not all sleep." The Bible often uses the word sleep to mean that someone has died. Paul expects that the dead will be raised "imperishable" and we, that is, we who have not "slept," or died, will be changed as well. He expects that those alive at Christ's coming will be changed and will take on new bodies–immortal bodies–but we will not have had to suffer death and so will not need to be resurrected! At Christ's return there will be only living people–some will have died and returned to life and others will never have died–but they will all be alive and in new bodies. Not only can we rejoice in the expectation of seeing Christ–which we should most eagerly await–but we can also rejoice in the expectation of seeing our Christian friends and family–and not only that, we can rejoice that we will be out of our old bodies and into new ones perfectly suited for life with Christ! The promise of a new body becomes more and more precious as you get older!

This encouragement was exactly what Paul tried to give the Thessalonians. There is a day to look forward to. It is a day not to miss–and God will see to it that it is not missed. Notice that Paul teaches that the Lord will descend with a shout, with the voice of an archangel, and with the trumpet of God. This combination: a shout, the voice of an archangel, and the trumpet of God, could serve both as a herald making an announcement, and as a summons to the dead to come out of their graves. It would seem to be both, as the dead all over the earth will come forth from their graves and all the living will rise to meet him in the air. In addition to knowing that these things will happen, we should be doubly confident that when they happen we will not be allowed to miss them.

Having established that the dead rise with eternal bodies, and that the living also are changed into equally perfect bodies, we might well ask, what next? What do we do with these new bodies, and especially for some, new bodies reunited with their souls? Our main passage for this chapter, 1 Thessalonians 4:13-18, tells us the answer. Specifically, verse 17 says, "Then we who are alive, who are left, will be caught up together with them in the clouds to meet the Lord in the air, and so we will always be with the Lord."

All Christians will be *caught up* into the air to *meet* Christ. Verse 17 contains two action verbs: "caught up" and "meet." We will look at both of these in a little more detail.

To be "caught up" means to be seized, or snatched; to be taken by force. It is translated from the Greek into our English Bibles with each of these words. There is an element of violence associated with being caught up. That is not to say it is something to be feared–but simply that it takes considerable force–humanly speaking–to lift a body suddenly off the earth and up into the clouds! And it will not be just one body but probably millions!

Notice how the word is used in the passage describing Philip and the Ethiopian eunuch,

> And he commanded the chariot to stand still: and they both went down into the water, both Philip and the eunuch; and he baptized him. And when they came up out of the water, the Spirit of the Lord caught away Philip; and the eunuch saw him no more, for he went on his way rejoicing (Acts 8:38-39).

Philip's ministry to this man was complete and the Lord immediately "caught him up" and he disappeared from sight. God put him down in another place where he was to serve. This "catching up" happened quickly—with force—but Philip was not harmed.

Jude instructs his readers "save others by *snatching* them out of the fire" (Jude 1:23). These are presumably sinners heading for hell and in need of drastic rescue—he uses the same word that is translated as "caught up" in our passage. They are close to the fire—it is almost too late—but Jude commands that they be caught, snatched, taken by force in a last minute rescue!

Paul himself had to be rescued by force at one point in his life. He was on trial before the council for his missionary efforts. The mob became angry and he was almost torn to pieces. He had to be caught up, or snatched away by force, by the guards to save his life (Acts 23:10).

Our being caught up to meet the Lord is nothing short of a rescue. We are in a dangerous world. We expect the work of the Antichrist to intensify. We expect Christians to face greater and greater persecution. We expect more and more so-called Christians to fall away and to abandon their faith. This world will get increasingly difficult for pilgrims and strangers to inhabit. To be caught up from it, to be with the Lord, to see evil judged, and to live forever in perfect bodies is a rescue we should look forward to.

The second action verb we will look at is the verb "to meet." This is the Greek word *apantesis*. This form of the word is used in only two other places in the Bible. It means more than we usually mean in

English when we use the word "meet." We frequently refer to someone we "met" at work or church, or we might tell someone we will "meet" them after supper at the ball-field. This is the usual meaning of the word meet in modern English. It means to come together. However, the word used by Paul in the original Greek is a rather technical term with a very specific meaning. It refers to the welcome given a visiting dignitary by a special party or delegation. The welcoming party would meet (apantesis) the honored guest near the end of their journey and escort them to their final destination. The word-picture is of believers (the resurrected and those who never died) meeting Christ in the air and escorting him on the final stage of his journey to earth. He is the "visiting dignitary" and we are the welcoming party in Paul's metaphor. You have probably seen something similar when the Queen of England gets out of a limousine in front of Buckingham Palace. Uniformed men rush to meet her, roll out a red carpet, and formally escort her inside. Something similar happens sometimes when Marine One, the U.S. Presidential helicopter, lands at the White House on a ceremonial occasion. It will be very helpful to look at the other two uses of this word in the Bible and their context to confirm this meaning.

The first usage of the word we will consider occurs in the book of Acts. A considerable portion of this book is devoted to recording Paul's missionary travels. Approximately ten chapters are spent describing his trip to Rome. In chapter 19 he resolved in the Spirit to reach this important city: "I must also see Rome" (v. 21). In Chapter 28 we see that he finally arrived. It was his destination and he would not be deterred. In fact, in Acts 23:11 we are told that the Lord himself, Christ, stood by Paul at night and told him he would testify in Rome. For ten chapters we follow Paul on his endeavors, his setbacks, and successes. He survived mobs, unfair trials, a plot to assassinate him, a shipwreck, and a poisonous snake bite. Nonetheless, he resolved to continue.

In Acts 28:15-16 we read of him reaching his destination. But to our question at hand we also read *how* he was received when he arrived. Luke, the writer of the book of Acts, writes,

> And the brothers there, when they heard about us, came as far as the Forum of Appius and Three Taverns *to meet* us. On seeing them,

Paul thanked God and took courage. And when we came *into* Rome, Paul was allowed to stay by himself, with the soldier that guarded him (emphasis added).

The brothers in Rome had been keeping an eye out for Paul. They knew he would be coming; they were expecting him. He was to be their honored guest. When they knew he was close they sent a special welcoming party out to meet him and escort him on the final leg of his journey to Rome. Notice that this passage not only uses the phrase "to meet," the exact Greek word used to describe meeting Christ in the air, but it also illustrates its meaning perfectly. Note that the welcoming party was from Rome, Paul's destination, and they went out. They left their city and went out to meet Paul who was still on his journey. After meeting him they escorted their honored guest into Rome, his destination. Could you imagine them doing anything else? Could you imagine Paul being turned away from Rome after all he had been through to get there? It is this same type of welcome that Paul says we believers will give to Christ when he comes. We will be the special welcoming party and he will be as the honored dignitary. We will meet him in the air and be his special escort on the final leg of his coming. Like the believers who met Paul, we are to be watching and waiting.

Interestingly, as in the passage concerning Christ's second coming and our meeting him in the air, the believers first *heard* that Paul was coming, then *saw* him. First, the brothers heard about Paul. Then they saw him.

The only other usage of the Greek word *apantesis* (to meet) is in Matthew 25 in what is called the parable of the wise and foolish virgins. The point of the parable is to be ready for Jesus' return. The context of the story is a wedding. The virgins in the story are somewhat like bridesmaids of today. And in the day when Jesus told this story the husband-to-be, the bridegroom, was the focus of attention, not so much the bride as is the case today. In today's weddings we play "Here Comes the Bride;" in their culture the song might have been "here comes the bridegroom." Read verses 1-10 carefully. Don't forget to observe how the words "to meet" are used.

Then the kingdom of heaven will be like ten virgins who took their lamps and went *to meet* the bridegroom. Five of them were foolish, and five were wise. For when the foolish took their lamps, they took no oil with them, but the wise took flasks of oil with their lamps. As the bridegroom was delayed, they all became drowsy and slept. But at midnight there was a cry, "Here is the bridegroom! Come out *to meet* him." Then all those virgins rose and trimmed their lamps. And the foolish said to the wise, "Give us some of your oil, for our lamps are going out." But the wise answered, saying, "Since there will not be enough for us and for you, go rather to the dealers and buy for yourselves." And while they were going to buy, the bridegroom came, and those who were ready went in with him to the marriage feast, and the door was shut.

Notice again that the point of the story is to be ready for the Lord's return. We need to live in such a way that we will not be ashamed of our lives and actions if he should return and find us doing the things we do. Like good servants we need to be about the Master's business no matter how long he is delayed. And the parable does indicate he was delayed and some people grew weary from waiting. Christians, on the contrary, need to be ready, to be eagerly expecting him–true Christians will want to be with him.

But our purpose in looking at this passage is to examine the phrase "to meet." Notice it is used twice in this passage. As in the case with Paul and the Christians in Rome, the events of the story actually illustrate the meaning of the word. Notice the virgins hear a cry announcing the arrival of the honored guest. Evidently someone was watching–as in the case with Paul–and as should be the case with us. The wise virgins served as a welcoming party and went out–out of the banquet hall where the wedding was to be held–met the guest of honor, then escorted him on the final leg of his journey into the banquet hall for the marriage feast. He received the "red carpet" treatment. His arrival was announced, he was met with an official delegation from the wedding, and he was escorted in as the guest of honor. Notice also, as with Paul, the bridegroom finished his journey into the wedding hall. Nothing could deter him–the virgins could not have turned him away–he could not have been sent back to his home or to his parent's home–he had a purpose–a destination–and he fully intended to accomplish that purpose.

We can return now to our main verse for this chapter and examine how it teaches that Christians will meet the Lord in the air when he returns. When Paul wrote that we will meet the Lord in the air, the meeting he described is like the Christians meeting him as he approached Rome or the wise virgins meeting the groom as he approached the wedding. Notice again the relevant events from verses First Thessalonians 4:16-17:

> For the Lord himself will descend from heaven with a cry of command, with the voice of an archangel, and with the sound of the trumpet of God. And the dead in Christ will rise first. Then we who are alive, who are left, will be caught up together with them in the clouds *to meet* the Lord in the air, and so we will always be with the Lord. Therefore encourage one another with these words. (emphasis added)

As with the bridegroom's coming, a cry goes forth when the Lord returns. In the case of Paul arriving in Rome the Christians "heard" about Paul. A party of Christians went out to welcome Paul and a party of virgins went out to meet the bridegroom. A party of Christians will go out to meet their Lord. The Christians accompanied Paul on the final stage of his journey to Rome. The virgins escorted the bridegroom on the last portion of his trip to the wedding hall. Likewise, we Christians will meet and welcome Christ in the air and be his escort on the final phase of his journey–his coming.

The only aspect of this comparison we have not addressed is just where he is coming to? Paul went to Rome and the bridegroom went to the wedding hall. Just as Paul would not be deterred from Rome, and the bridegroom would not be deterred from his wedding, Christ will not be deterred from his destination either! He is coming to the earth–he will not be turned around and sent back to heaven with his mission uncompleted! Imagine Paul struggling against all his obstacles (shipwreck, stoning, false trials, mobs) only to be deterred by the brethren within sight of Rome!

Or the bridegroom, who waited perhaps for many months or even years to marry his beloved, perhaps he even paid a large dowry to her father (a sum of money or items of value)–only to have the virgins send him back to his home without being married. This would be absurd! Of course Christ intends to finish his journey–of course he is an honored dignitary–of course we are his escort–of course he finishes his journey and makes it to the earth. It is a second "coming," not a second "going." And when he comes, and we see him, and we meet him, we can look forward to being with him forever! It is no wonder Paul said we should comfort one another with these words. This prospect can take the sting out of any pain, any loss, any setback, or disappointments we may experience in this life. We will one day see and hear and be with our Lord, never to be separated again.

Application: Are you looking forward to the Lord's return? I mean really longing for it? Are you regularly thinking of him or are your thoughts confined to this world and the treasures found here? Are you living in a way that you would not be ashamed of if Christ were to return today? Are there sins you need to repent of? The foolish virgins were out of oil for their lamps. They were not prepared for the bridegroom's arrival. They had gotten weary. He came. He and the wise virgins went in to the wedding. The door was shut and the others were left out. Only the wise enjoyed the marriage supper. Are you wise? Will you enjoy the presence of Christ forever?

CHAPTER 10

The Judgment, Part 1:
The Judge, the Accused, and the Accusations

We have discussed the major aspects leading up to Christ's second coming and the key events that take place upon his arrival to the earth. The dead will have been raised. The living Christians (including those recently resurrected) will have risen in the air to meet the Lord, and Christ will have completed his second coming to the earth. This chapter will look at a major activity that occurs soon after Christ arrives on the earth. We will explore the judgment. The judgment is often considered an unpleasant subject–and it certainly is for the unbeliever. But it need not be so for the Christian. Recall our summary of the order of events.

**Coming → dead rise → living rise → meet in the air →
Christ judges → eternity begins**

We will pursue our study of the judgment through a series of questions. We will ask the *who* and *what* questions in this chapter, and the *when, where,* and *why* questions in the next two chapters. We will of course see that there are two sides to some of these questions. For example, we may ask *who* is the judge, and we may also ask who *is being judged.* As with the other topics we've discussed, this subject has very practical applications. As we shall see, we will all face a judgment in one way or another–it can be a time of terror followed by eternal punishment–or a time of blessing followed by eternal joy. As you read, you might ask yourself which it will be for you.

Who is the Judge?

The role of judge is primarily committed to the Son. We say primarily because there is a sense, and Scripture to support it, that the Father also has a role. But we will focus on the Son as this is what I believe the Bible does.

Perhaps the clearest passage indicating that Jesus is the judge is found in John 5:22. Jesus himself says, "The Father judges no one, but has given all judgment to the Son."

Paul is also very clear as to the identity of the judge, "For we must all appear before the judgment seat of Christ, so that each one may receive what is due for what he has done in the body, whether good or evil" (2 Corinthians 5:10). It is the judgment seat *of Christ.* Christ is pictured here as courtroom judge seated and ready to conduct business. If you have ever been in a courtroom and watched a judge enter and take his seat you know it is an impressive sight. There is an air of solemnity. He may greet people as he enters–perhaps say a word or two–but once he takes his seat he is ready to engage in serious matters–and everyone in the courtroom knows it. Paul pictures Christ as taking such a seat.

Luke records Paul's words to the men of Athens concerning the judgment of Christ:

> The times of ignorance God overlooked, but now he commands all people everywhere to repent, because he has fixed a day on which he will judge the world in righteousness by a man whom he has appointed; and of this he has given assurance to all by raising him from the dead (Acts 17:30-31).

The man appointed to judge is the man who was resurrected from the dead. In his first coming Jesus came as a suffering servant. He washed feet. He received abuse. He was laughed at and scorned. He was spit upon. He was insulted with a mock trial. He was killed. But his death was not the end. He was resurrected, and his resurrection, Paul says, is assurance that he is the One, the man of God's own choosing, the One who will return. When he returns he comes as the Judge. It will be radically different than the first coming. He will receive no abuse, no scorn, no mocking–he will come as a judge with all authority. None will laugh, none will scorn, none will spit, none will mock.

This Judge however, will not judge alone. He will have assistants. Jesus himself taught that the angels will play a role in the judgment. Consider the following passages.

> Just as the weeds are gathered and burned with fire, so will it be at the close of the age. The Son of Man will send his angels, and they will gather out of his kingdom all causes of sin and all law-breakers, and throw them into the fiery furnace. In that place there will be weeping and gnashing of teeth (Matthew 13:40-42).

> Then will appear in heaven the sign of the Son of Man, and then all the tribes of the earth will mourn, and they will see the Son of Man coming on the clouds of heaven with power and great glory. And he will send out his angels with a loud trumpet call, and they will gather his elect from the four winds, from one end of heaven to the other (Matthew 24:30-31).

We will discuss the nature of the judgment shortly, but from what we have seen so far it should be clear that the role of angels is clearly different from the role of Jesus. They are assistants—they help but they are not the ones making the final decision. Notice in the first passage the angels are helping to gather "all causes of sin" and all "law-breakers" and casting them into punishment. We will see soon that one result of the judgment is punishment.

In the second passage above we also see the angels sent out, but this time they are sent to gather his elect from the four winds. The angels go about the whole earth to gather God's people. These are the ones who are doing the master's will when he comes (verse 46). They are not cast into the fiery furnace as are the law-breakers—they will be blessed and be extremely happy with the result of the judgment.

Who *will be judged?*

We have seen clearly that Christ is the judge. We will look briefly now at who will be judged by him. One of the clearest passages indicating who will be judged is the well known passage concerning the sheep and the goats. The word-picture Jesus uses to describe the judgment of the wicked and the righteous is that of a shepherd separating sheep from goats. In his metaphor sheep represent the righteous and goats represent the wicked. Jesus, of course, is the shepherd presiding over this process.

> When the Son of Man comes in his glory, and all the angels with him, then he will sit on his glorious throne. Before him will be gathered all the nations, and he will separate people one from another as a shepherd separates the sheep from the goats. And he will place the sheep on his right, but the goats on the left. Then the King will say to those on his right, "Come, you who are blessed by my Father, inherit the kingdom prepared for you from the foundation of the world." Then he will say to those on his left, "Depart from me, you cursed, into the eternal fire prepared for the devil and his angels." And these will go away into eternal punishment, but the righteous into eternal life (Matthew 25:31-34, 41, 46).

It is well worth reading this entire passage. The portions of this passage that were omitted from the above quotation concern "what" is judged and will be discussed below.

This judgment passage clearly indicates that the Judge, the Son of Man, will be on his throne separating the wicked from the righteous. Both groups will be present. They will have been brought here to this judgment ultimately by the power of God, but also by the angels acting on God's behalf, as we have just seen. The people at the judgment will be from all the nations. It will not be limited to only some very wicked nations or to only those most righteous nations—but all the nations will be present. The wicked will be there. The righteous will be there. Everyone who has ever lived will be there—all at the same time. Some will be alive when Christ comes because they have not yet died. Others will have died but have been resurrected at his coming. All will face this judgment—there will be no escape—not even death will allow someone to miss this.

Notice there will be no in-between classes of people there. There are no half sheep/half goats receiving some in-between result from the judgment. There will be no middle ground. Jesus was clear throughout his ministry–you are either for me or against me (Luke 11:23). And it is the same at the judgment. There will be no second chance after this point. There will be no class of people who were almost good enough and get a little more time to get it right. There will be no more time to make up some missed assignments or perform good works. There will be no changing the mind of the Judge. There will be no appeal to a higher court. The cleverest attorney will be of no use here. There will be no jury to manipulate. His ruling is *the* ruling and it is final and irreversible.

Notice the finality of the language used. The wicked go away into eternal punishment and the righteous into eternal life. There is no chance to change one's eternal condition after this point. It will be too late for anyone to get serious about life and sin and matters of importance after this point. The judgment is pronounced and the eternal consequences begin.

These things are reinforced by Paul in Romans 2:1-10:

> Therefore you have no excuse, O man, every one of you who judges. For in passing judgment on another you condemn yourself, because you, the judge, practice the very same things. We know that the judgment of God rightly falls on those who practice such things. Do you suppose, O man–you who judge those who practice such things and yet do them yourself–that you will escape the judgment of God? Or do you presume on the riches of his kindness and forbearance and patience, not knowing that God's kindness is meant to lead you to repentance? But because of your hard and impenitent heart you are storing up wrath for yourself on the day of wrath when God's righteous judgment will be revealed. He will render to each one according to his works: to those who by patience in well-doing seek for glory and honor and immortality, he will give eternal life; but for those who are self-seeking and do not obey the truth, but obey unrighteousness, there will be wrath and fury. There will be tribulation and distress for every human being who does evil, the Jew first and also the Greek, but glory and honor and peace for everyone who does good, the Jew first and also the Greek.

He teaches that each one will be judged (v. 6) and that the judgment will include both Jews and Gentiles (v. 9) and all who sinned, whether before or after the law was given (v. 12). None shall escape. As with the sheep and the goats, the wicked, according to Paul, will face wrath and fury, while the righteous look forward to an eternity of life, glory, honor, and peace. There is no escape–all will face this judgment. It can be something to fear, or something to long for.

Additionally, it is worth noting that fallen angels will also be judged. In fact, they are even now being kept in gloomy darkness reserved for the day of judgment (2 Peter 2:4, Jude 1:6). Note especially the passage from Jude, "And the angels who did not stay within their own position of authority, but left their proper dwelling, he has kept in eternal chains under gloomy darkness until the judgment of the great day." In addition to teaching that angels will face judgment, this passage calls our attention to the fact the judgment will be on "the great day." We will come back to this topic later.

What is being judged?

We have already seen that the judgment involves the separation of the wicked and the righteous. It is the beginning of an eternity of torment in hell for some, and the beginning of an eternity in joyful bliss for others. By way of comparison, it is the sentencing phase to a modern courtroom and trial. The ruling and punishment are delivered and the sentence is begun immediately. Unlike a trial in a modern courtroom, however, *this* Judge arrives knowing the verdict! He knows the righteous from the wicked–he knows his followers from the followers of the Evil One. He will not need convincing. He will not need to hear carefully constructed arguments. He will not need to be persuaded or convinced into ruling a certain way or understanding the facts in a certain light. He knows the facts–all of them–and understands them perfectly. In this section we will take a look at *what* is being judged. It may not be what you think!

CHAPTER 10: *The Judgment, Part 1*

In the Matthew 25 passage we used above to show *who* was being judged, we intentionally omitted the part of the passage that showed *what* will be judged. Now we need to focus our attention on those verses.

"For I was hungry and you gave me food, I was thirsty and you gave me drink, I was a stranger and you welcomed me, I was naked and you clothed me, I was sick and you visited me, I was in prison and you came to me." Then the righteous will answer him, saying, "Lord, when did we see you hungry and feed you, or thirsty and give you drink? And when did we see you a stranger and welcome you, or naked and clothe you? And when did we see you sick or in prison and visit you?" And the King will answer them, "Truly, I say to you, as you did it to one of the least of these my brothers, you did it to me." Then he will say to those on his left, "Depart from me, you cursed, into the eternal fire prepared for the devil and his angels. For I was hungry and you gave me no food, I was thirsty and you gave me no drink, I was a stranger and you did not welcome me, naked and you did not clothe me, sick and in prison and you did not visit me." Then they also will answer, saying, "Lord, when did we see you hungry or thirsty or a stranger or naked or sick or in prison, and did not minister to you?" Then he will answer them, saying, "Truly, I say to you, as you did not do it to one of the least of these, you did not do it to me" (Matthew 25:35-45).

Notice that what is being judged are the things that people *did* or *did not do!* The righteous, who inherit the kingdom according to the previous verse, are commended for giving a drink, giving a welcome, clothing the naked, visiting the sick, and visiting those in prison. The wicked, by contrast, are sent away into eternal fire along with the devil and his angels because they did not provide food and drink to the hungry and thirsty, did not welcome the stranger, clothe the naked, and visit the inmate. It is clearly the things people did that are brought forward in the judgment.

In a clear parallel account of the judgment in Revelation 20:12, the vision shows the books being opened and the dead being judged by what was written in the books, specifically according to what they had done. This passage describes the same judgment where the devil and the wicked ones are thrown into the lake of fire, their eternal punishment where they are tormented day and night forever (v. 10). The righteous, by contrast, have their names written in the book of life and enjoy the eternal blessing detailed in the twenty-first chapter of Revelation.

Paul reinforces this idea with an admonition to aim to please the Lord. He says, "So whether we are at home or away, we make it our aim to please him. For we must all appear before the judgment seat of Christ, so that each one may receive what is due for what he has done in the body, whether good or evil" (2 Corinthians 5:9-10). We receive what is due for what we have done "in the body."

In addition to our actions, the judgment covers everything we say. Jesus himself warned that on the Day of Judgment we would all give an account for every careless word we speak (Matthew 12:36). Do you answer back to your mom disrespectfully? Do you argue needlessly with your brothers or sisters? Do you speak unkind words to that boy or girl you are not so fond of? How about those things you mutter under your breath when you don't like the way circumstances turn out? You will give an account of these things!

If somehow we could control our actions and control our words we would be okay, right? Wrong! On the Day of Judgment God judges the *secrets* of men! Our secrets, like our actions, are judged by Christ (Romans 2:16). When the Lord comes to judge our secrets, he will also disclose the "purposes of the heart" (1 Corinthians 4:5). The purposes of the heart are the motives, or the reasons why people do the things they do. God sees and knows why you do something! Are you doing good only to be noticed and praised by other people? God sees through it. Do you say "yes" to your mom but fully intend to disobey? Do you do what dad asks but without a cheerful heart? God sees your heart! He judges not just the outside act–but he judges why you do what you do. On the other hand, sometimes you mean well and things don't turn out the way you intended. Despite your best, well-intentioned efforts to do good sometimes things beyond your control prevent the good that you intended from happening. God sees this too. Paul wrote to the Romans (1:13) that he had intended to visit them but was thus far prevented. God saw that Paul meant well. He sees that you mean well when you do. He judges your intentions.

A Note of Caution

The previous section explains from Scripture that the judgment will bring forward the works people have done. This is clearly taught from the passages selected above as well as many more that could be added to them. The Bible is clear on this fact. However, this is not all the Bible has to say concerning the outcome of the judgment. To say that one's works are judged ought to raise questions in your mind. Hopefully you have been taught that salvation is based on grace and on grace alone! Surely you have heard that that one is saved and brought to Christ through faith and faith alone! One cannot work their way into heaven. No one except Christ can be good enough to earn heaven. No one can commit so many good works as to overcome their sins and "bad works." But if these things are true, how can the judgment be focused on works?

To be sure, one is saved and made right with God on the basis of God's grace, through faith, both of which are God's free gift—unearned by man. The child of God is given a new heart, with new motives, and becomes, in fact, a new creature. However, can you see someone's new heart? Can you see a physical change in the appearance of the person who has become a Christian? Do they look different? No, they do not have a new physical appearance. You cannot see their heart to know that it is different. But what you do see is a change in their behavior. What they do and what they want to do are changed. You see a change in the way they speak. You see a change in the way they act and respond to other people. You cannot see their motives and secret intentions as God does, but you can see the *results* of their new motives in the way they now live. The Bible refers to our behavior and the things we do as our fruit. Jesus taught that a tree is known by its fruit (Matthew 12:33). The fruit can be good or bad. As in the case of an apple tree we do not see the sap and sugars in the stem of the tree. We do not know that the root contains all the necessary ingredients to produce a good apple until it actually *does* produce a good apple. Then we know it's a good tree. The final fruit it bears is the evidence that the tree is good, that the root is good, and that the "insides" of the tree are good and working properly.

Likewise, a person is known by his "fruits;" his actions and his words. People do not see our hearts but they hear the things our hearts lead us to say. They see the fruit we produce–either good works or bad. They form their opinion of us, or we might say they form their judgment of us, by what they see and hear on the outside. In the courtroom of heaven, at the judgment, the things we have said and done in our lives are brought forth as *evidence* to show that we are either sheep or goats. Those watching the judgment (everyone) will not be able to see the heart. They will only be able to see the evidence or proof that the heart produces. The good works we may have done do not make us into sheep– they do not make us "not guilty" in this trial–they are merely the outside evidence used to show what is true on the inside.

Look carefully at the Matthew 25 passage concerning the sheep and the goats. When the Judge comes in his glory to judge, the first thing he does is separate the sheep from the goats. Only after this is done is there any discussion about their works. He arrives with a judgment in hand. There is no debating, no presentation of evidence, no deliberating–sheep are sheep and goats are goats. The evidence concerning feeding the hungry and clothing the naked come later and it comes only to support the judgment that has *already been made* based on one's relationship to Christ. Jesus knows his people. He knows them now and he will know them in the day he comes to judge. On the outside Christians and non-Christians look alike in their physical appearance. The difference is on the inside. Since you cannot see the inside, God uses the works people do to show that they *are* different on the inside.

Application: Are you showing the fruits that indicate you are a child of God, that you have a new heart? Paul lists the following fruits in Galatians 5:22-23: love, joy, peace, patience, kindness, goodness, faithfulness, gentleness, self-control. In the passage we looked at earlier from Matthew, Jesus indicated that some fed the hungry, clothed the naked, visited the sick–and some didn't. No one earned a favorable judgment by doing these things–this simply showed that these individuals had changed hearts–they had hearts that *wanted* to do good, that had a desire to do the things God desires. Do you desire these things? Do you have a desire to obey God? Will the evidence brought forth on the Day of Judgment show you to be a sheep–or a goat?

CHAPTER 11

The Judgment, Part 2:
Timing and Location

In the last chapter we answered questions concerning the identity of the judge, the identity of the people being judged, and the identity of what is being judged. In short, Christ is the Judge, all people will face the judgment, and our deeds, thoughts, and secret motives will be judged. In this chapter we will ask the *when* and *where* questions concerning the judgment.

When is the judgment?

The Bible is very clear that the judgment occurs on the last day. However, it uses several different literary terms to refer to this day. For example, some passages refer directly to the "last day," others to "that day," or "an hour," others to the "end of the age." Still others tie the judgment to other events occurring on the last day, such as the return of Christ or the resurrection. In this section we will look at a variety of these references to show that the Biblical writers speak with one voice when it comes to the timing of the judgment.

We'll begin with a couple of the most direct, straightforward statements concerning this important topic. John quotes Jesus as saying,

> If anyone hears my words and does not keep them, I do not judge
> him; for I did not come to judge the world but to save the world.
> The one who rejects me and does not receive my words has a judge;
> the word that I have spoken will judge him *on the last day*. And I

know that his commandment is eternal life. What I say, therefore, I say as the Father has told me" (John 12:47-50, emphasis added).

These words of Jesus confirm that there will be a judgment, it will be by the words of Jesus, and it will be on last day. This judgment will impact those who reject me. By contrast however, those who accept God's commandment can expect eternal life. As we saw before, the judgment is the dividing line between this life and eternity. There is no turning back. The judgment is pronounced and the consequences are forever.

Recall that we had previously established the fact that the resurrection would be on the last day. "No one can come to me unless the Father who sent me draws him. And I will raise him up on the last day" (John 6:44). John links these two events, the judgment and the resurrection, together on the last day. Notice the words of Jesus that John records in chapter 5:

> For as the Father has life in himself, so he has granted the Son also to have life in himself. And he has given him authority to execute judgment, because he is the Son of Man. Do not marvel at this, for an hour is coming when all who are in the tombs will hear his voice and come out, those who have done good to the resurrection of life, and those who have done evil to the resurrection of judgment (John 5:26:29).

Here John refers to an *hour* when those in the tombs hear his voice and come out to face judgment. Whether this implies that the judgment only lasts an hour or simply that there is an hour when it begins we cannot say. But it is clear that this hour is closely tied to the point in time when Jesus returns and the dead rise. Notice that in this hour *all* those in the tombs hear his voice and come out. The righteous will face a resurrection of life, and the evil a resurrection of judgment.

The apostle Paul teaches that the judgment will be on "that day" and he also ties it to the return of Christ. In Romans 2 he issues some stern warnings for his readers. The first 16 verses are very helpful to an understanding of this issue. It would be wise to read them before reading further in this book.

In Romans 2 Paul has indicated that men will face judgment. He asks, rhetorically, if these people really believe they will escape the judgment (v. 3). Then in verses 5-8 he says,

> But because of your hard and impenitent heart you are storing up wrath for yourself on the *day of wrath* when God's righteous judgment will be revealed. He will render to each one according to his works: to those who by patience in well-doing seek for glory and honor and immortality, he will give eternal life; but for those who are self-seeking and do not obey the truth, but obey unrighteousness, there will be wrath and fury. (emphasis added)

Paul indicates the judgment will be on the day of wrath. There is one, coming, final and unavoidable day when all will be judged. It is "the day," the day of wrath for the wicked. Some go to eternal life, others to eternal wrath and fury. Since the conditions after this are eternal, this has to be the last day. There can be no other day after the last one! This day leads to heaven or hell–there can be no turning back. There will not be one more day to get things right. There can be no others. This explains Paul's urgency in trying to get his readers to repent. There will be no such opportunity after the Day of Judgment. By the last day, the last chance will have passed.

We will look at one other passage to confirm that the judgment will be on the last day. The apostle Peter draws an interesting contrast between the "last days" and the "last day." Look at what he says in 2 Peter 3:3-7:

> Knowing this first of all, that scoffers will come in the last days with scoffing, following their own sinful desires. They will say, "Where is the promise of his coming? For ever since the fathers fell asleep, all things are continuing as they were from the beginning of creation." For they deliberately overlook this fact, that the heavens existed long ago, and the earth was formed out of water and through water by the word of God, and that by means of these the world that then existed was deluged with water and perished. But by the same word

the heavens and earth that now exist are stored up for fire, being
kept until the day of judgment and destruction of the ungodly.

Peter expects that scoffers and skeptics will come in the last days
questioning whether or not Jesus will come back. Those who
doubt the claims of Christianity were predicted two thousand years
ago! They will specifically question whether Jesus is actually
returning or not. These people deliberately over look the facts (v.
5). Peter continues in verse 7, "But by the same word the heavens
and earth that now exist are stored up for fire, being kept until the
day of judgment and destruction of the ungodly." Notice that the
day of judgment awaiting these people results in their destruction.
If on this day the wicked are destroyed it is clearly their last day. It
is not only the end of the wicked, however, but the earth and
heavens are being "stored up for fire." Beyond this we can expect
a new heavens and a new earth (v. 13), about which we have much
to say in later chapters. For now, it is sufficient to say that the
concept of the new heavens and new earth are what the righteous
can expect in eternity. If eternity follows the day of judgment, it
must be the last day of this life.

In a previous chapter we looked at the parable of the tares and the
wheat and discussed how all of time is now divided into this age and
the age to come. After this age we enter the age to come–what we
refer to as heaven or hell. Our purpose in that chapter was to point
out that Jesus' second coming was the end of this age and the
beginning of the age to come. In this chapter we will look again at
that parable and confirm that his return not only marks the dividing
point between this age and the age to come, but that the judgment
actually punctuates the beginning of the age to come. After Jesus
told the parable to the crowds he later explained it to his disciples.
Here are his words of explanation from Matthew 13:37-43.

> He answered, "The one who sows the good seed is the Son of Man.
> The field is the world, and the good seed is the sons of the
> kingdom. The weeds are the sons of the evil one, and the enemy
> who sowed them is the devil. The harvest is the close of the age, and
> the reapers are angels. Just as the weeds are gathered and burned
> with fire, so will it be at the close of the age. The Son of Man will

send his angels, and they will gather out of his kingdom all causes of sin and all law-breakers, and throw them into the fiery furnace. In that place there will be weeping and gnashing of teeth. Then the righteous will shine like the sun in the kingdom of their Father. He who has ears, let him hear."

Notice again that Jesus describes this harvest as occurring at the close of the age. At this point in time, the weeds, or sons of the evil one, are gathered by the angels and cast into the fire. In the fiery furnace there will be weeping and gnashing of teeth. This is hell–their final state. By contrast, the righteous will shine like the sun in God's kingdom. These two classes of people, the weeds and the wheat, are very much like the sheep and the goats. The goats were sent away into eternal fire and punishment, the righteous to eternal life. Again, the judgment separates the two classes of people and sends them to their eternal destination. There is no turning back. No day follows the Day of Judgment. There is no opportunity to change your relation to Christ after this point. It is final. It is the last day.

We will look at one additional passage to confirm that the Day of Judgment is the final day of this life and of this earth. Paul was writing to the Thessalonians to encourage them in their suffering and persecutions. He reminds them that the coming of the Lord and his judgment on their enemies will give them eternal relief. Note his words.

This is evidence of the righteous judgment of God, that you may be considered worthy of the kingdom of God, for which you are also suffering–since indeed God considers it just to repay with affliction those who afflict you, and to grant relief to you who are afflicted as well as to us, *when the Lord Jesus is revealed from heaven with his mighty angels in flaming fire*, inflicting vengeance on those who do not know God and on those who do not obey the gospel of our Lord Jesus. They will suffer the punishment of *eternal destruction*, away from the presence of the Lord and from the glory of his might, when he comes on *that day to be glorified* in his saints, and to be marveled at among all who have believed, because our testimony to you was believed (2 Thessalonians 5:1-10, emphasis added).

Suffering saints can expect that those who persecute them will one day be punished. This suffering will continue until the Lord is revealed from heaven–his second coming–and will result in their eternal destruction. It will be on that day, when he comes to be glorified. Again, this time in the words of the apostle Paul, we see that the judgment results in the wicked being sent off into eternal consequences. After the judgment they will have had their last day in this life. The judgment will therefore be on their last day. Jesus will be glorified and marveled at among those who believed. This means of course, that in order to marvel at Jesus we will have to be with him! We will be with him and the wicked will have been sent away. The righteous and the wicked will forever be separated at this point. As Paul says, we will have relief. The wrongs committed against God's children will eventually be avenged. They will be dealt with. In the meantime, take heart! Our suffering has a purpose. It helps us to be "considered worthy of the kingdom of God." Even though we are saved by grace, our suffering will be used as evidence in the judgment that we are sons of God. It will not be in vain. Consider yourself fortunate to suffer as a Christian!

Where is the judgment?

The Bible provides less detail to answer this question than it does the previous ones we have addressed. However, some of the passages we have already looked at give us some clues. In general, the idea of a judgment associated with the second *coming* would indicate that the judgment will be at the place Jesus *comes to*.

For instance, the passage we just considered from 2 Thessalonians 5:1-10 indicates that the Lord will be revealed from heaven and will inflict vengeance on those who persecute his people. The word "from" seems to indicate he will be leaving the place where he is now and going somewhere else. He is not being revealed in heaven but from heaven. The fact that the passage also adds that this happens when he comes on that day would seem to indicate that he will be arriving on the earth. You use the word come to describe someone leaving one place and traveling to the place where you are located. For example, you might say that your grandparents will come to see you for your birthday. It is reasonable for people hearing you say this to understand that they will arrive at the place you live on that date. There would be no reason for someone to conclude that they will be meeting you somewhere else unless you gave more information. Likewise, this text doesn't clearly say Jesus will hold the judgment on the earth– but the writer simply says he will come and execute vengeance on his enemies who are on the earth. Interestingly, the wicked will then be sent away into eternal destruction. This also implies that until they receive their sentence they remain where they were before the judgment, that is, on the earth. The righteous, by contrast, are not sent away, but are granted relief. The righteous remain on the earth–which we will discuss later.

In the Matthew 25 passage concerning the sheep and the goats we see the same things taught. This passage begins when the Son of Man comes in glory. Again, it is emphasized he leaves where he is now and comes here. When he comes and judges, the sheep simply inherit the kingdom. They remain in place and receive blessings. The wicked by contrast, pictured as goats, are sent away. They are told to depart into eternal fire.

He teaches the same in the parable of the sower in Matthew 13. In verses 42 and 43 the wicked are thrown but the righteous will remain and shine like the sun in the kingdom of their Father. The righteous remain where they are–the earth–but the wicked are cast away.

These passages seem to strongly imply that the judgment will be on the earth. There does not appear to be a passage that clearly and simply comes right out and says it. However, it is clear that the judgment under consideration happens when Jesus comes, that is, when he leaves where he now is and arrives somewhere else. The way we use the word come indicates that the person in question will be relocating to where we are. Following the judgment, the righteous remain where they were before the judgment, and the wicked are sent away. Away from where? Presumably, away from the earth.

Application: Jesus describes the close of this present age with these words, "The Son of Man will send his angels, and they will gather out of his kingdom all causes of sin and all law-breakers, and throw them into the fiery furnace. In that place there will be weeping and gnashing of teeth. Then the righteous will shine like the sun in the kingdom of their Father. He who has ears, let him hear" (Matthew 13:41-43). Do you have ears to hear? Are you listening to the Judge?

CHAPTER 12

Why There Will Be a Judgment

We have seen that there will be a judgment on the last day, the day of the Lord's return, and that it will evidently be on the earth. As we have stressed, there are two and only two outcomes. God's enemies will face a judgment of death and weeping and gnashing of teeth; his children will face a judgment of life in which they will "shine like the sun." We will conclude our discussion of the judgment by asking why it is necessary. We will look at six reasons.

Why will there be a judgment?

There are numerous reasons why there will be a judgment. Some have been alluded to in verses we've already examined. I suspect if you thought about it you could come up with a list of your own! Many of the reasons God will hold a judgment are similar to reasons there are "mini-judgments" on the earth all the time. We have made comparisons to courtrooms and the judgments that take place there daily. There are judgments at your home when mom or dad settles a dispute between you and your brother or sister. There are judgments after certain athletic events. While athletic "judgments" are a little different from what we have been discussing, there are some similarities as well, as we shall see. Why do we have judgments? We shall attempt to answer this question.

First, common sense tells us we are accountable for our actions. When we do well, we typically receive praise from our parents or from someone in authority. When we do wrong we receive some sort of consequence. It is the same with God. We are all accountable for all we do, and say, and think. Remember that Jesus said that on the Day of Judgment we will be expected to give an account of every word we speak (Matthew 12:36) and every thing we do (Matthew 25:35-36). Paul adds that Christ will also judge our secrets (Romans 2:16). We must give an account. We have been given life, time, and resources. We are like the servants in the parable Jesus related in Matthew 25. Our master has gone away for a long time. But when he returns he comes to "settle accounts" (v. 19). In the parable two did well and were called good and faithful servants. They were told to "enter into the joy of your master" (21, 23). One was a wicked and slothful servant. He wasted what God had given him and was "cast into outer darkness" (25, 30). God calls us to account. We are responsible for the time and opportunities God has given.

The second reason there will be a judgment is that God will punish his enemies and the enemies of his people. You realize, of course, that *his* enemies and the enemies of *his* people are one and the same group of people. Christians are hated because of Christ (John 15:18, Luke 6:22). When the Lord returns he does so to punish all his enemies. They will give an account, then receive their punishment. Notice the passage from 2 Thessalonians 1:8-9 we discussed earlier:

> ...the Lord Jesus is revealed from heaven with his mighty angels in flaming fire, inflicting vengeance on those who do not know God and on those who do not obey the gospel of our Lord Jesus. They will suffer the punishment of eternal destruction, away from the presence of the Lord and from the glory of his might.

He will "inflict vengeance on those who do not know God and who do not obey the gospel." Vengeance means retribution, or revenge. These people deserve dire and lasting consequences for their sins and they will receive it. They have lived the lives of sinners, they do not know God, and have not responded properly to the gospel of Jesus Christ. God will take vengeance on them! This is no mere slap on the wrist like the trivial punishments handed out by many of our courts today. In this world people commit crimes and get away with them. Not so in God's courtroom. Nothing and no one escapes his eye. He is not detached and uninterested—he is personally involved. The ones

Jesus punishes with eternal destruction are ones who rejected him. It is a personal matter. His person and his word have been rejected and abused. He is personally involved. Those who committed sins against other people committed sins against him (remember the sheep and the goats). They committed sins against the "least of these." The Judge himself knows the facts. He knows the crimes, the sins, the wicked words and thoughts of those who stand accused. No one will be hidden from his sight (Hebrews 4:13). He has been wronged. Those who have wronged him will suffer the consequences.

It may be impossible to overstate the intensity with which the Bible emphasizes this point. God will have vengeance. He is patient now, but when that day comes he will pour out his wrath. Notice what Scripture says:

> Beloved, never avenge yourselves, but leave it to the wrath of God, for it is written, "Vengeance is mine, I will repay, says the Lord" (Romans 12:19).

> The LORD is a jealous and avenging God; the LORD is avenging and wrathful; the LORD takes vengeance on his adversaries and keeps wrath for his enemies (Nahum 1:2).

> I will execute great vengeance on them with wrathful rebukes. Then they will know that I am the LORD, when I lay my vengeance upon them (Ezekiel 25:17).

> Put to death therefore what is earthly in you: sexual immorality, impurity, passion, evil desire, and covetousness, which is idolatry. On account of these the wrath of God is coming (Colossians 3:5-6).

> But by the same word the heavens and earth that now exist are stored up for fire, being kept until the Day of Judgment and destruction of the ungodly (2 Peter 3:7).

We are never to seek revenge on our own. It belongs to God and to God alone. We can be certain that it will happen. "I will repay," God says. He will deal justly with his enemies. He will punish their immorality. He will pour out wrath on those who have evil desires and practice idolatry. He will destroy the ungodly. It will be for them the worst thing imaginable. They would prefer to have mountains fall on them. Notice what is said in the book of Revelation concerning God's enemies,

> [*they were*] calling to the mountains and rocks, "Fall on us and hide us from the face of him who is seated on the throne, and from the wrath of the Lamb, for the great day of their wrath has come, and who can stand?" (6:16-17).

They will face his wrath, his vengeance. The Lamb is not a suffering servant here. He is not portrayed as meek and lowly at the judgment. He is in plain view before his enemies and he is displaying his wrath. Vengeance is his, and he will have it on that Day.

There is a third reason there will be a judgment. When God judges the wicked this action brings relief to his children. Notice again the passage from 2 Thessalonians 1 we looked at earlier concerning judgment on the wicked. In verses 6 and 7 Paul makes it clear that the judgment comes in part because it is what they deserve, but also in part to grant relief to his children who suffer.

Since indeed God considers it just to repay with affliction those who afflict you, and to grant relief to you who are afflicted as well as to us, when the Lord Jesus is revealed from heaven with his mighty angels.

God considers it just to *repay* those who afflict you and to grant *relief* to you who are afflicted. Like a loving father God notices the sufferings of his children! He is involved in our day-to-day lives. He takes note of the evil and unkind things people say and do to you. We need not worry. We need not "keep score." Our loving Father sees all and knows all and will repay with vengeance those who do not repent. His judgment will bring us relief from our enemies!

A fourth reason for the judgment is that it will mark the time when his children are rewarded. We will not go into great detail concerning all the Bible has to say about our reward, or rewards, as Christians. However, in answer to the question that we ask, "Why is there a judgment?," we need to address the rewards that will be given to the righteous.

Just as the judgment brings vengeance to the wicked and relief to the righteous, so it also brings loss to unrepentant sinners and rewards to those who are forgiven. The basis of our reward or our loss is whether or not we have built our lives around Christ. Notice what Paul teaches,

> For no one can lay a foundation other than that which is laid, which is Jesus Christ. Now if anyone builds on the foundation with gold, silver, precious stones, wood, hay, straw–each one's work will become manifest, for the Day will disclose it, because it will be revealed by fire, and the fire will test what sort of work each one has done. If the work that anyone has built on the foundation survives, he will receive a reward. If anyone's work is burned up, he will suffer loss, though he himself will be saved, but only as through fire (1 Corinthians 3:11-15).

God will disclose the real nature of everyone's work. If you have built on the foundation of Christ and worked to build his kingdom you will have built something that matters. You will receive a reward. Notice when this testing will take place–the Day. On the day when Jesus returns and all people stand before him to give an account he will reward those who have done as their Master commanded. Jesus himself taught that you may be hungry now, you may weep now, you may be persecuted and mocked now because of Christ, but "Rejoice in that day, and leap for joy, for behold, your reward is great in heaven" (Luke 6:21-23).

We must give a word of caution in order to keep this idea of a reward in perspective. While the above passage teaches that *we* are building on the foundation of Christ–and we are called to do just that, we must also remember that it is all grace–it is all part of God's free gift that we are able to work for him. On our own we would choose to work for sin and wickedness. God could accomplish what he wants to do without you or me. He chooses to involve us in his plan–he chooses, in love and in grace–to allow us to participate in the work he is doing. It is true we work. It is true we receive a reward. But we must remember that the reward is ultimately traced back to God's grace–his free gift through his Son. In Colossians 3:24 our reward is referred to as an inheritance. An inheritance is something a son or daughter receives from their parents when their parents have died. The son or daughter does not earn an inheritance–they receive it simply because they *are* a son or daughter. Our greatest reward is to be forgiven and to be rightly related to Christ. He is our greatest reward–he is the pearl of great price. Whatever else our rewards may involve, when Jesus comes at the judgment those who are his children receive him as an inheritance. We are united with him forever–never to be separated. This is what heaven is all about.

The fifth reason for the judgment is God's glory. The glory of God seems to be an all-but-forgotten topic in our day but it is important to God–and to the Biblical writers. John wrote in Revelation 14:7, "And he said with a loud voice, 'Fear God and give him glory, because the hour of his judgment has come, and worship him who made heaven and earth, the sea and the springs of water.'" There will be glory associated with God at the judgment. People will see Christ as he is, in all his splendor and all his glory. He will not be coming as a meek and lowly servant. He will not be coming to wash feet, to be taunted or to receive abuse. He will be coming as king and as judge. It will be blissful for his children, fearful for his enemies–and glorious to all. Those who refused to give him glory while they lived in this life will be put to shame.

Sixth, and finally, we see that there is a judgment because of sin. While this may be obvious from the fact that God will judge his enemies and will hold all accountable for their actions, it needs to be said clearly and directly. God has been patient with sinners. For thousands of years during the Old Testament days people would sin and seem to get away with it. On occasion God would punish the wicked nations that abused the Jews or strike some individual that had committed very serious sins, especially if they had done so in public. But there seemed to be far more sin in the world than there was punishment. A casual observer might wrongly conclude that God was not serious about sin. He might reason that since most people appeared to sin and get away with it that God wasn't really concerned after all. God endured these false accusations or beliefs about himself for thousands of years. Then came the cross. God demonstrated clearly for all to see that he is serious about sin and will punish it. On the cross Christ took the punishment for the sins of his people. On the Day of Judgment, the wicked will take the punishment for their own sins.

Application: Despite the appeal of the cross, most will continue in their sin and unbelief. God commands people everywhere to repent (Acts 17:30). He does not beg people to repent. He does not suggest it. He does not present it as a good idea to consider. The God who created you *commands* you to repent. Will you? Most will not. On that day most will be brought to the judge against their will. They will hear the awful words "depart from me" as did the goats. Some few will obey. Some will hear his voice and by his grace they will believe. Will you obey Christ and repent? Will you seek him as a reward? The day is coming.

CHAPTER 13

Hell–Unending Torment

The previous chapters on the judgment focused on the who, what, when, where, and why of the judgment. Several of the passages referred to eternal life or eternal destruction. These could be said to be the *results* of the judgment. Following the judgment people will find themselves in the state they will be in for all eternity. We refer to these states, or places, as heaven and hell. The Bible has more to say about heaven than it does about hell. Heaven is a far more pleasant topic about which to read (and write!) than is hell. Nonetheless, hell is real. The Bible teaches about hell and so we must spend some time discussing it.

We are not given detailed descriptions of hell. The passages and phrases that describe hell are usually brief. As you might expect, most of the Bible is written for the benefit of those who will believe it. Those who repent and turn to Christ need not be overly concerned with what hell is because they will never be there. The descriptions about hell do serve to warn people. These glimpses into hell are like warning signs along a dangerous road. They tell of a place to be avoided at all costs. They are reminders of the consequences of being God's enemy. They encourage unrepentant sinners to seek relief where it may be found. They are warned to flee from the "wrath to come."

You may have noticed the many jokes and lighthearted ways people speak of hell and of death. People often make light of things they are uncomfortable with. And hell certainly makes people uncomfortable. You have surely seen cartoons depicting the devil laughing about some twisted scheme or prank he planned to play on people in hell. Aside from the fact that the devil is not in charge in hell, people like these cartoons because they take their minds off of a very serious and frightening subject. Sinners have guilty consciences. Paul teaches that even those who have not read or heard God's law are accused by their conscience (Romans 2:15). You know what it feels like to have done something wrong and to feel terrible about it. The only relief is to repent and apologize for it. But those who do not repent are left with guilt and with the nagging knowledge that there will be an accounting. They make light of hell. They tell jokes that make them feel better. But as we will see there is nothing funny about hell. No jokes and no cartoons can hide the horribleness of hell. In this chapter we will look at only five aspects of hell. We will consider hell as being a place of fire. This is probably most people's conception of hell. But hell is also described as outer darkness, gloomy chains, a place where there is weeping and gnashing of teeth, and a place of destruction.

The Bible frequently refers to hell as a place of fire. Notice Jesus' description in the Sermon on the Mount, "But I say to you that everyone who is angry with his brother will be liable to judgment; whoever insults his brother will be liable to the council; and whoever says, 'You fool!' will be liable to the hell of fire" (Matthew 5:22).

Recall what we said about the judgment being concerned with words, actions, and even thoughts. A sin as simple as calling your brother a fool is sufficient to send a person to hell–a hell of fire. I'm sure you've been burned before one way or another. You've touched a hot stove, spent too long in the sun, or burned yourself with a match or around a campfire. You know how badly it hurts. A bad burn can be one of the most painful types of injuries. It is unpleasant to think about. Hell is described as a place of fire. Your sin is ultimately against God, and God, as we saw in the last chapter, will have vengeance on his enemies. They enemies will suffer a suffering that is described as a hell of fire.

This suffering is not brief. It is unending. The Bible describes it as an unquenchable fire. It cannot be put out. This torment is to be avoided at all costs. Jesus taught that we should undertake extreme measures in this life to avoid hell in the age to come. "And if your hand causes you to sin, cut it off. It is better for you to enter life crippled than with two hands to go to hell, to the unquenchable fire" (Mark 9:43). The fire is unquenchable. It cannot be stopped. An ocean of water could not cool it down. It will burn forever–and burn those forever who are cast there.

Following the judgment, the devil and his followers will be cast into hell as well. This is recorded in the book of Revelation where hell is described as a lake of fire. This lake burns with sulfur.

> And the beast was captured, and with it the false prophet who in its presence had done the signs by which he deceived those who had received the mark of the beast and those who worshiped its image. These two were thrown alive into the lake of fire that burns with sulfur (Revelation 19:20).

> And the devil who had deceived them was thrown into the lake of fire and sulfur where the beast and the false prophet were, and they will be tormented day and night forever and ever (Revelation 20:10).

Interestingly, the text notes that they will be thrown alive into this place where they will endure and unending torment, day and night. They will be alive and see it coming. In the moments before being throne here the wicked will know their doom. They will know they are receiving the proper consequences for their actions. They would prefer to have mountains fall on them but they will have no such relief (Revelation 6:16).

Hell is also a place of destruction. Jesus asked his hearers to keep in mind the distinction between those who have authority over the body in this life but have no control over the soul in the life to come. He said, "And do not fear those who kill the body but cannot kill the soul. Rather fear him who can destroy both soul and body in hell" (Matthew 10:28). In Jesus' comparison of the Christian path with the path of the world, he used the analogy of a narrow gate and wide gate. We are encouraged to enter by the narrow gate that leads to life (Matthew 7:13). Most, however, will choose the wide gate that leads to destruction. The soul and the body are destroyed in hell. Hell is a place of destruction.

At this point you may be wondering, how hell can be a place of unending torment and a place of destruction? That's a good question! On one hand it seems the torment of the flames never ends, and on the other it seems that the Bible says someone comes to an end by being destroyed. The apparent problem is the way we understand the word destroy. We think of it meaning that the body will cease to exist, that the person destroyed will be no more. But this cannot be the case for many passages teach that the punishment is eternal (think of the goats in Matthew 25:36). When the Bible speaks of hell as being a place of destruction it means it is a place of *unending* destruction. The state of being destroyed will go on forever. A person's body and their soul will go on and on being ruined. If the wicked were simply destroyed quickly and never suffered after that, the punishment would be relatively easy by comparison. But this is not the case. They are forever trapped in a state of fire and torment and of being continually destroyed. The wicked in hell will wish they could be destroyed in the sense that we normally use the word. They will certainly wish the destruction would be final. However, they will be raised in the resurrection with new bodies that will be perfectly suited for suffering. They will survive unending destruction. They will continue to be destroyed forever and ever.

Understandably, this fire will also cause incredible torment. This torment will cause weeping and gnashing of teeth. In the parable of the sower, Jesus taught that the wicked will be gathered out of his kingdom and cast into hell:

> The Son of Man will send his angels, and they will gather out of his kingdom all causes of sin and all law-breakers, and throw them into the fiery furnace. In that place there will be weeping and gnashing of teeth (Matthew 13:41-42).

Jesus regularly emphasized this aspect of hell. In the parable of the wicked servant who beat his fellow servants, we see the same consequence. This servant thought that the master (Christ) would be delayed in his coming. He behaved wickedly and was caught. The expectation was that the master would return and "cut him in pieces and put him with the hypocrites. In that place there will be weeping and gnashing of teeth" (Matthew 24:51).

The phrase "weeping and gnashing of teeth" conveys a sense of extreme pain. We tend to bite down hard with our jaw or even grit our teeth when something hurts us. You may have seen documentaries or movies about the Civil or Revolutionary Wars and observed the horrid pictures of the battlefield following a bloody battle. In some cases an arm or leg was wounded so badly it could not be healed and had to be sawn off to save the rest of the body. The soldier would have to be restrained. It might take several men to hold him down. Then, he would be given a rag or perhaps a lead bullet to bite down on to focus his attention away from the pain. He bit furiously on the bullet during the pain.

We see animals do the same thing when they have been wounded or caught in a trap. Perhaps you have been warned to stay away from wounded dogs or other animals. In their pain they often bite uncontrollably. They may gnaw at their own leg. They may bite their own master or snap about at the air. The behavior appears irrational–but seems to be a widely observed response to extreme pain.

Perhaps you bite down or grind your teeth after smashing your shin into a table–or as your dad digs a large splinter from the sole of your foot. Unfortunately for the wicked, this is only a small taste of what they will face forever in hell. Circumstances will be so bad there will be constant tears and constant gnashing of teeth. To say it will be unbearable is an understatement. It will be unbearable and without end.

Perhaps the worst of hell however, is not the pain. It is not the fire and not the unending destruction. The worst may be that people will be forever away from the Lord. Paul stated that "They will suffer the punishment of eternal destruction, away from the presence of the Lord and from the glory of his might" (2 Thessalonians 1:9). Paul is describing the eternal punishment that awaits the evil persons who persecute God's children. To call it eternal destruction is not enough. To further clarify the horrific nature of this judgment Paul adds the phrase, *away from the presence of the Lord and from the glory of his might.* This is a horror of horrors. One cannot imagine what it is to be totally and helplessly away from the presence of the Lord. We take his presence for granted. Even the wicked in this life benefit from the presence of the Lord. They may not admit it, but they have no idea what it would be like without him.

This separation from the Lord is also compared to gloomy darkness (2 Peter 2:4). Peter teaches that fallen angels are presently being kept in chains and in "gloomy darkness" awaiting the day of judgment. The main thrust of the passage is that he knows how to punish the wicked and it will be worse than imaginable. The evildoers being described by Peter can expect comparable punishment. Hell is like being bound in chains in a gloomy place. The word gloom conjures ideas of darkness, depression and loneliness. Even now these angels have a taste of what it will be like to be held away from the Lord.

Where the Lord is not found there is also darkness. Notice the parable of the servants and the talents.

> For to everyone who has will more be given, and he will have an abundance. But from the one who has not, even what he has will be taken away. And cast the worthless servant into the outer darkness. In that place there will be weeping and gnashing of teeth. When the Son of Man comes in his glory, and all the angels with him, then he will sit on his glorious throne (Matthew 25:29-31).

The wicked servant will be cast into outer darkness. This is a somewhat violent act. He will be thrown out with a force he cannot fight or overcome into a place of outer darkness. No one would knowingly choose such a place. People may laugh at hell or even make jokes about how fun it will be to be there and engage in unending wickedness. However, the Bible pictures no one going there by choice. They are always thrown there or cast there with force. None will go willingly once they see it coming. This outer darkness away from the Lord further contributes to weeping and gnashing of teeth (Matthew 22:13). It is horrible beyond imagination.

Application: The Bible says nothing pleasant about hell. It is to be avoided at all costs. None would choose to go there if they understood what it will be like. Nonetheless, it is what sinners deserve. The wages of sin is death (Romans 6:23) and that involves an eternal death, an eternal destruction, and on-going torment. But God has provided a way of escape. Go to Christ. Seek forgiveness, for as the wages of sin is death, the gift of God is eternal life in Christ Jesus our Lord. Whoever believes is not condemned but has eternal life (Romans 8:1).

CHAPTER 14

Heaven, Part 1:
Is it Heaven, or is it God?

The next four chapters will discuss the concept of heaven. This will be much more pleasant than the previous chapter! There are many misconceptions about heaven. People have ideas about heaven from picture books, from movies, commercials on television, and from jokes and stories they've heard. Unfortunately, many of these ideas are not consistent with what the Bible teaches. We will spend this chapter discussing a few concepts about heaven that may be new to you.

First, heaven is practically synonymous with God. This means that "God" and "heaven" mean essentially the same thing in many places in the Bible. We conclude this because certain writers in the Bible use these two terms in identical contexts to mean the same thing. Notice how Mark and Matthew use these terms in the parable of the sower. I encourage you to read the entire context of this parable and convince yourself that in both cases Matthew and Mark are recording the same teaching of Jesus. Only part of the parable will be included below:

> And when he [Jesus] was alone, those around him with the twelve asked him about the parables. And he said to them, "To you has been given the secret of the kingdom of God, but for those outside everything is in parables, so that they may indeed see but not perceive, and may indeed hear but not understand, lest they should turn and be forgiven." And he said to them, "Do you not understand this parable? How then will you understand all the parables? The sower sows the word" (Mark 4:10-14).

Mark refers to the Kingdom of God. He was very direct with his audience. In the kingdom of God the sower is an evangelist or witness. He spreads the word of God. Some who hear the word believe it and it bears fruit in their lives. Others are distracted by the cares of this world or blinded by the devil. Matthew relays the same parable of Jesus but uses a different term for the kingdom. See if you catch it:

> He put another parable before them, saying, "The kingdom of heaven may be compared to a man who sowed good seed in his field, but while his men were sleeping, his enemy came and sowed weeds among the wheat and went away. So when the plants came up and bore grain, then the weeds appeared also" (Matthew 13:24-26).

Matthew tells the same story and has the same characters—but he refers to the kingdom of heaven instead of the kingdom of God! Matthew's Jewish audience would have likely been offended at so open a use of God's name and so he used a synonym in place of the word "God."

Jesus tells one story about the kingdom. He is telling one story about how the word of God is spread. The story has one main point, and that is how the word is received by the hearers and why it either bears fruit or doesn't. There are not two kingdoms; the writers simply use different words to mean the same thing. When Matthew's readers read "heaven" they would think "God." They would not think of a place, a condition, or some state of being. To them heaven meant God. We speak the same way in our culture. For example, we may refer to "The President" of the United States. We may also refer to the same person as the "commander-in-chief." In either case there would be no difference in what we meant or the story we told about this person. People would clearly understand these were simply two names for the same person. The first century audience reading the books of Matthew and Mark would likewise have understood that God and heaven were both used to mean "God."

This is by no means an isolated example. We see this throughout the parables. Read how Matthew and Mark relate the parable of the mustard seed:

> He put another parable before them, saying, "The kingdom of heaven is like a grain of mustard seed that a man took and sowed in his field. It is the smallest of all seeds, but when it has grown it is larger than all the garden plants and becomes a tree, so that the birds of the air come and make nests in its branches" (Matthew 13:31-32).

> And he said, "With what can we compare the kingdom of God, or what parable shall we use for it? It is like a grain of mustard seed, which, when sown on the ground, is the smallest of all the seeds on earth, yet when it is sown it grows up and becomes larger than all the garden plants and puts out large branches, so that the birds of the air can make nests in its shade" (Mark 4:31-32).

There can be no doubt this is the same parable. Jesus is telling the same story in each case. Matthew, for his Jewish audience, substitutes the word heaven for the word God. Matthew is writing under the inspiration of the Holy Spirit. He is not taking an inappropriate liberty with the words of Jesus. God directed him to make this substitution. Matthew is writing in such a way as to keep the text from being needlessly offensive to some of his readers but God is teaching the reader something about himself.

In the parable of the prodigal son Jesus reflects this truth. Take note of the repentant son's confession:

> And he arose and came to his father. But while he was still a long way off, his father saw him and felt compassion, and ran and embraced him and kissed him. And the son said to him, "Father, I have sinned against heaven and before you. I am no longer worthy to be called your son." But the father said to his servants, "Bring quickly the best robe, and put it on him, and put a ring on his hand, and shoes on his feet" (Luke15:20-22).

The son confessed that he had sinned against heaven! If heaven is simply a place, some region of space as is commonly believed, how is it that it can be sinned against? It could not be. The point is that the son, in this parable, had sinned against his earthly father and against God. When Jesus told the story he had the son confess his sin as being against heaven. His hearers would have clearly understood that the son sinned against God. Again, we see the word heaven used to mean *essentially* the same thing as the word God.

It will be helpful to look at one more usage of the word heaven as a substitute for God. You will remember that the second commandment forbids taking the name of the Lord in vain (Exodus 20:7). This means you do not swear in anger using God's name, speak lightly or jokingly with God's name, or use it in any careless way. However, if you have studied the names of God you will know he has many names. But not only does he have many names, he also has synonyms for his names. He is a diverse and multifaceted God and requires a diversity of names. Jesus taught this truth in a rebuke to the Pharisees. They were swearing oaths by the altar or the temple and then attempting to evade the promise they had made by some technicality or loophole. Perhaps you have heard children make a promise then claim they had their fingers crossed and so do not have to keep their promises. Jesus rebuked this way of speaking and thinking,

> So whoever swears by the altar swears by it and by everything on it. And whoever swears by the temple swears by it and by him who dwells in it. And whoever swears by heaven swears by the throne of God and by him who sits upon it (Matthew 23:20-22).

Jesus says that if you swear by heaven you swear by the throne of God and thus by God himself who sits on the throne. In other words, to swear by heaven is to swear by God.

Obviously it is possible to use the word temple or the word throne in a way that does not refer to God. There are many instances where the word temple refers to a physical building. (But even so, in the ultimate sense of the word the Lord is the temple as well, Revelation 21:22.) The word heaven likewise can be used to refer to the atmosphere around the earth or to the starry sky. It certainly *can* mean the physical space above the earth. But many of the other

New Testament uses of the word clearly indicate God, or the presence of God, or something that comes from God.

The two concepts of God and heaven are not identical, but we can say that in many uses they are essentially the same. In addition to the words being used interchangeably by Jesus and the writers of the New Testament, we see throughout the whole Bible that heaven is depicted as God's special dwelling place. Heaven is wherever God is. His very presence makes heaven. He is the focus of heaven. This is made clear in a number of passages.

The LORD is in his holy temple; the LORD's throne is in heaven; his eyes see, his eyelids test the children of man (Psalms 11:4).

The LORD looks down from heaven; he sees all the children of man (Psalms 33:13).

Thus says the LORD: "Heaven is my throne, and the earth is my footstool; what is the house that you would build for me, and what is the place of my rest? (Isaiah 66:1)

In the thirtieth year, in the fourth month, on the fifth day of the month, as I was among the exiles by the Chebar canal, the heavens were opened, and I saw visions of God (Ezekiel 1:1).

And he [Stephen] said, "Behold, I see the heavens opened, and the Son of Man standing at the right hand of God" (Acts 7:56).

God is the focal point of heaven. When the heavens opened to a person such as Stephen or Ezekiel they see God. They see God on his throne. It is God who makes heaven heaven. Those prophets and apostles who have had visions of heaven have been impressed and consumed first and foremost with the presence of God. He makes heaven what it is. When Jesus taught us to pray his model prayer began "Our Father in heaven" (Matthew 6:9). The two are so linked as to be essentially inseparable. You cannot think of one without the other. It is this Person we desire to spend eternity with, not the place itself.

Furthermore, heaven is not only where God is but it is where God is in his glory. When the heavens were opened at Stephen's stoning he "gazed into heaven and saw the glory of God, and Jesus standing at the right hand of God" (Acts 7:55).

In John 17:24 Jesus prayed specifically for those people the Father had given him. "Father, I desire that they also, whom you have given me, may be with me where I am, to see my glory that you have given me because you loved me before the foundation of the world." He prays that they may be with him and that they may see his glory. Heaven is where Christ is, but specifically it is where Christ is in his glory. Heaven seems to be specifically associated with Christ and his glory and his presence. In John 6:33 and 38 Jesus is described as the bread of life who came down from heaven. It was his presence that made the kingdom of heaven at hand or nearby (Matthew 3:2, 4:17, 10:17). He was later taken back into heaven (Acts 1:9-11). We await his return from heaven (1 Thessalonians 1:10). Heaven is where Christ is.

Many of us need to reconsider how we think about heaven. We have become accustomed to thinking about heaven primarily as a place. And while it is a place in one sense, the Bible indicates that it is primarily about a Person. The Bible rarely, if ever, says Christians "go to heaven" when we die. Instead, it says we go to be "with Christ." Being with Christ is the essence of heaven. This is a subtle but very important difference. Our hope for the future is not so much a nice place to go, but the real joy of heaven is that we get to be with Christ. Our fuzzy thinking about heaven keeps many of us from looking forward to it as we ought. Far too many people think of heaven in terms of floating on clouds strumming harps and singing with angels all day! These images came from television and not from the Bible. They obscure clear thinking about heaven. It is hard to get excited about the television concept of heaven. It is not hard, however, to get excited about spending eternity with Christ. Christ himself was motivated by the prospect of having his people with him. Notice how Jesus thought about these things.

Father, I desire that they also, whom you have given me, may be with me where I am, to see my glory that you have given me because you loved me before the foundation of the world (John 17:24).

And if I go and prepare a place for you, I will come again and will take you to myself, that where I am you may be also (John 14:3).

Jesus desires that his people be with him. He wants us to be with him and to see his glory. Our hope ought to be the same as his. If his desire is that we be with him, our desire ought to be with Christ. Jesus even prepares a place for this to happen! Heaven is that place, but it is not primarily a place. The essence of heaven is not a place, but the person. The place would be nothing without the Person. In fact, as was said in the last chapter, the absence of God is the essence of hell. It is his presence that makes a place heaven.

Paul expressed these same ideas in very vivid terms.

For to me to live is Christ, and to die is gain. If I am to live in the flesh, that means fruitful labor for me. Yet which I shall choose I cannot tell. I am hard- pressed between the two. My desire is to depart and be with Christ, for that is far better. But to remain in the flesh is more necessary on your account (Philippians 1:21-24).

His desire is to depart his body (to die!) and be with Christ. Paul is not longing for heaven. He does not simply desire to go and be somewhere better. He desires to be with Christ.

Paul's thinking was consumed with the idea of being with the Lord. He was painfully aware that while on this earth he was physically away from the Lord. He longed to be with Christ. Observe the stark contrasts in Paul's thinking:

So we are always of good courage. We know that while we are at home in the body we are away from the Lord, for we walk by faith, not by sight. Yes, we are of good courage, and we would rather be away from the body and at home with the Lord (2 Corinthians 5:6-8).

We Christians are either "away from" or "at home with" the Lord. These are the two options for Paul. Paul was not clinging to this life. He was content to be here as long as this is where God wanted him, but he knew that to be with Christ in person was far better. He would rather be at home with the Lord.

The thought of being with God comforted Paul and he said it should comfort us. We previously discussed Christ's return and our meeting him in the air. The end result of this meeting is that we would always be with him. Recall Paul's words,

> For the Lord himself will descend from heaven with a cry of command, with the voice of an archangel, and with the sound of the trumpet of God. And the dead in Christ will rise first. Then we who are alive, who are left, will be caught up together with them in the clouds to meet the Lord in the air, and so we will always be with the Lord. Therefore encourage one another with these words (1 Thessalonians 4:16-18).

Paul does not say we will be in heaven forever. He does say we will always be with the Lord. This is not a minor difference! How can this not excite us? Encourage one another with these words.

Application: Do we think the way Paul did? Are our thoughts regularly directed to Christ? When you think of heaven do you think of being with Christ? If our thoughts of the life to come are vague, if they are unfocused, if we think in terms of some nebulous place in outer space then our thoughts are not Biblical thoughts. Repent of these things! Think of being with Christ. Think of being with your Savior. Think of being with the One who gave you life and ransomed you from death. Think of the One presented in the pages of Scripture and of being with him.

CHAPTER 15

Heaven, Part 2:
Heaven is more like Earth than you Think

We spent the last chapter making the point that heaven is not so much a place as it is a person. In this chapter, we will make the case that heaven *is* a place! Are we arguing against ourselves? Not at all! The Bible emphasizes that the key aspect of heaven is Christ. Christ's presence is what makes heaven, heaven. We discussed the near oneness of God and heaven. Recall the parallel uses of "kingdom of God" and "kingdom of heaven"? The two are so linked as to be inseparable. So while we spent a chapter making the point that heaven is not *primarily* a place, we will look at the fact that it nonetheless *is* a place.

God himself made this perfectly clear in Isaiah 57:15:

> For thus says the One who is high and lifted up, who inhabits eternity, whose name is Holy: "I dwell in the high and holy place, and also with him who is of a contrite and lowly spirit, to revive the spirit of the lowly, and to revive the heart of the contrite."

God dwells in a place. He occupies space that is high and holy. He is infinitely above us. He is set apart. He is altogether holy. He is all these things, and yet, astonishingly, he also dwells with the lowly in spirit. He is with the humble. We see in this verse God occupying heaven as his special dwelling place–high and lifted up–apart from men–and yet we see him in another sense dwelling with men, helping us, comforting us, sustaining us in times of need. God is everywhere, especially with his people, and most especially in heaven.

The Psalmist expresses his desire and hope to be with God in this special place. David found comfort in having the Lord as his shepherd in this life. Yet he looked forward to being with the Lord in a more intimate way. He declared "Surely goodness and mercy shall follow me all the days of my life, and I shall dwell in the house of the LORD forever" (Psalms 23:6). David anticipated the day in which he would be with God in a place he described as a house.

Jesus illustrates this point as well. He prepares a place where he can be with his people:

> In my Father's house are many rooms. If it were not so, would I have told you that I go to prepare a place for you? And if I go and prepare a place for you, I will come again and will take you to myself, that where I am you may be also (John 14:2-3).

We see in these two short verses both the truth we illustrated in the last chapter and the point we are making now. Jesus is preparing a place–but it is a place where we can be with him. He does not call it heaven. The emphasis is on being together.

Given that heaven is a place, you may well wonder what sort of a place it is. You may be asking what it will look like and what we will do there. These are understandable questions. Many people have them! It is hard for most of us to get excited about "heaven" when we understand so little of it. In this and the next chapter we will look at what the Bible says about heaven. It may surprise us.

The Bible teaches that the concept of heaven is and always has been an earthly one. From the earliest days and events recorded in the Bible we see that the idea of eternal life with God involved land–it involved the earth and the physical stuff of the earth with which we are familiar. The book of Job and the events in it are believed to be among the oldest in the Bible. Job knew that after his death he would see the Lord. Interestingly, he also knew he would see the Lord on the earth.

> For I know that my Redeemer lives, and at the last he will stand upon the earth. And after my skin has been thus destroyed, yet in my flesh I shall see God (Job 19:25-26).

Job not only expected to have died but he expected his body to have been decomposed–his flesh destroyed. You may recall we discussed this verse in an earlier chapter to teach the bodily resurrection. In addition to proving a resurrection, Job notes that his new body will see God–and God will be standing on the earth. This will be after Job has a new body. It will therefore be after the resurrection that occurs at the return of Christ. Job's expectation was that he would have his resurrected, eternal body and be with God on the earth.

Job of course is not the only Old Testament saint to have such an expectation. One cannot think of Abraham and not think of his expectations to inherit a "land."

> And I will establish my covenant between me and you and your offspring after you throughout their generations for an *everlasting* covenant, to be God to you and to your offspring after you. And I will give to you and to your offspring after you the land of your sojournings, all the land of Canaan, for an *everlasting* possession, and I will be their God" (Genesis 17:7-8, emphasis added).

God promised Abraham the land of Canaan as an everlasting possession. He and his descendants would possess it forever. Twice in these verses God emphasized that it would be theirs forever. Did Abraham possess it forever? Did he possess it at all? He did not. In fact, he never really possessed any of it except a small burial site he had to purchase (Genesis 23:3-9). Did God's promise fail? Was there some sort of cosmic mistake? Not at all. Far more is meant than that Abraham will own a piece of land some time in his life.

Abraham himself did not think God's promise meant only that he would inherit a piece of land. He knew God meant something else entirely. Notice how Abraham understood God's promise according to the writer to the Hebrews.

> By faith Abraham obeyed when he was called to go out to a place that he was to receive as an inheritance. And he went out, not knowing where he was going. By faith he went to live in the land of promise, as

in a foreign land, living in tents with Isaac and Jacob, heirs with him
of the same promise. For he was looking forward to the city that has
foundations, whose designer and builder is God (11:8-10).

Abraham was looking beyond the land where he lived to a
heavenly city. He lived in a land of promise. It was to him a foreign
land. But he was looking forward to the city God had designed and
built. Hebrews tells us Abraham did this by faith. He and Isaac and
Jacob lived in tents in the land they would never own in this
lifetime. But they would own it! God's promise would not fail and
they knew it. They looked beyond the land and tents they saw with
their physical eye and saw, with the eye of faith, a better city, even
a better country.

> These all died in faith, not having received the things promised, but
> having seen them and greeted them from afar, and having
> acknowledged that they were strangers and exiles on the earth. For
> people who speak thus make it clear that they are seeking a
> homeland. If they had been thinking of that land from which they
> had gone out, they would have had opportunity to return. But as it
> is, they desire a better country, that is, a heavenly one. Therefore
> God is not ashamed to be called their God, for he has prepared for
> them a city (Hebrews 11:13-16).

If Abraham had been thinking of the land he had formerly lived in
he would have had the opportunity to return to it. But he wasn't
thinking of such a land. He was seeking a home–a new home–a
better country–even a heavenly one. Abraham did not think God's
promise had failed. He always understood it to be bigger and more
glorious than the land on which he walked. But it was and is an
earthly expectation. It was to involve land. It was to involve a
country. It was to involve a city. Interestingly, both Job's and
Abraham's idea of heaven is sounding curiously like earth!

In fact, an eternal earth is exactly what the Scriptures affirm from
cover to cover. Thousands of years after Job and Abraham, the
Psalmist echoed these ideas in poetry.

> As for me, I have set my King on Zion, my holy hill. I will tell of the
> decree: The LORD said to me, "You are my Son; today I have

begotten you. Ask of me, and I will make the nations your heritage, and the ends of the earth your possession" (Psalms 2:6-8).

Who is the man who fears the LORD? Him will he instruct in the way that he should choose. His soul shall abide in well-being, and his offspring shall inherit the land (Psalms 25:12-13).

In Psalm 25:13 the Greek word land also means earth. In some translations, such as the King James, the Greek word is actually translated as earth. Throughout much of the Old Testament you will see the words land and earth used interchangeably. God's people will inherit the land. They will inherit the earth. Fortunately for Christians today, these promises are not restricted to Abraham and his immediate family. Those who belong to Christ are counted as Abraham's children. The apostle Paul said this very clearly,

There is neither Jew nor Greek, there is neither slave nor free, there is no male and female, for you are all one in Christ Jesus. And if you are Christ's, then you are Abraham's offspring, heirs according to promise (Galatians 3:28-29).

Are you in Christ? Do you belong to him? Has he forgiven your sins? If so, you are Abraham's offspring! You are his descendants. You are his children—"according to his promise." This means that you, along with Isaac and Jacob, will inherit the land. You and all the rest of Abraham's family will inherit the earth. But be careful. Notice the condition Paul lays out in the Galatians passage above. You must first be in Christ. "If you are Christ's, then you are Abraham's offspring." *If* you belong to Christ, *if* you have been adopted into God's family, then in addition to this primary relationship you *also* become a member of Abraham's family. Abraham has done nothing for you. He only received God's promise. He received God's wonderful blessing by faith, the same way you must receive God's blessings. Neither you nor Abraham earned the blessing. We have no right to demand it. We receive it humbly, as the Psalmist also says, "But the meek shall inherit the earth; and shall delight themselves in the abundance of peace" (Psalms 37:11, KJV). This of course should be familiar, as it is exactly the same thing Jesus said: "Blessed are the meek: for they shall inherit the earth" (Matthew 5:5, KJV). Those who are Christ's are his because of his grace, his free unmerited favor. You could not make yourself be born into Abraham's family any more than you made yourself to be born into the family you were born into in this life. You enter this family by grace, through faith–and you must do so meekly. And if you do so, you shall inherit the earth for all eternity.

In addition to the patriarchs and the psalmists, we see the prophets expressing these same ideas.

> Your sun shall no more go down, nor your moon withdraw itself; for the LORD will be your *everlasting* light, and your days of mourning shall be ended. Your people shall all be righteous; they shall *possess the land forever*, the branch of my planting, the work of my hands, that I might be glorified (Isaiah 60:20-21).

> My servant David shall be king over them, and they shall all have one shepherd. They shall walk in my rules and be careful to obey my statutes. They shall *dwell in the land* that I gave to my servant Jacob, where your fathers lived. They and their children and their children's children shall dwell there *forever*, and David my servant shall be their prince *forever*. I will make a covenant of peace with them. It shall be an *everlasting* covenant with them. And I will set them in their land and multiply them, and will set my sanctuary in their midst *forevermore*. My dwelling place shall be with them, and I will be their God, and they shall be my people. Then the nations will know that I am the LORD who sanctifies Israel, when my sanctuary is in their midst *forevermore* (Ezekiel 37:24-28, emphasis added).

Look back at the two verses above. Notice the emphasis on the words forever and forevermore. God is not merely telling his people through the prophets that they will live some or even all of their life in a land. They will live in the land he gives them forever. More importantly however, as we emphasized before, it is not so much the land or the place that is important–it is being with Christ. We see that emphasized here as well. Notice here God says "My dwelling place shall be with them" and "my sanctuary is in their midst." God intends to be with his people in the land that he has given us (and will give us!). We will be with him forever.

Heaven will be Christ and his people together forever. Heaven may be more familiar than you think.

Application: Do you think about being with Christ? Do you have a reasonable expectation of being with him where he will spend eternity? Do you seek a better country? A heavenly one? If it is to be your inheritance you must receive it meekly. He dwells with those who have contrite hearts and lowly spirits. Go to Christ as a lowly sinner. Go to him now–while there is time.

CHAPTER 16

Heaven, Part 3:
A New Earth

We concluded the last chapter by saying that heaven is a place and that the Bible describes that place as both land and as the earth. God's people will inherit the land forever. The meek shall inherit the earth. But in what way could this present earth be a suitable place for heaven? Surely, *this* earth cannot be heaven! When we look around we see so much sin and corruption. We see death. We see people who do not love God. We see people who hate one another. We see wars, famines, sickness, and sadness. How can this be heaven? How can this be anything to look forward to?

The promises that God's people would inherit the earth are actually two-part promises. There is the promise of the earth–but it is specifically a promise concerning the *new* earth. Consider the witness of both the Old and New Testaments:

> For behold, I create new heavens and a new earth, and the former things shall not be remembered or come into mind (Isaiah 65:17).

> But according to his promise we are waiting for new heavens and a new earth in which righteousness dwells (2 Peter 3:13).

> Then I saw a new heaven and a new earth, for the first heaven and the first earth had passed away, and the sea was no more (Revelation 21:1).

God's people continue to have an expectation of inheriting the earth. This has not changed. But, like Abraham, we are not looking to this present earth, but to a new one. As we said above, this world is full of the problems caused by sin. We mentioned death and sickness. Think of the list Jesus gave in the Sermon on the Mount: wars, famines, and earthquakes (Matthew 24:8). There is Paul's list in Romans 1:29. People are full of "unrighteousness, evil, covetousness, malice, envy, murder, strife, deceit, maliciousness, and gossip." Countless more sins could be named. We have made this world a very unpleasant place.

We have so corrupted the earth with our sin that the earth itself longs to be made new! The Bible teaches that the earth, even the entire creation, was subjected to suffering because of the sin of man. The earth longs to be set free from this corruption and from its bondage to death and decay. Paul describes the earth as looking forward to the day when this happens, to the day when the children of God will have new bodies and be revealed for who we are. Read carefully what Paul says:

> For I consider that the sufferings of this present time are not worth comparing with the glory that is to be revealed to us. For the creation waits with eager longing for the revealing of the sons of God. For the creation was subjected to futility, not willingly, but because of him who subjected it, in hope that the creation itself will be set free from its bondage to corruption and obtain the freedom of the glory of the children of God. For we know that the whole creation has been groaning together in the pains of childbirth until now. And not only the creation, but we ourselves, who have the first-fruits of the Spirit, groan inwardly as we wait eagerly for adoption as sons, the redemption of our bodies (Romans 8:18- 22).

Paul is apparently using personification. He is giving human traits to the earth. The earth is said to be "longing" and "groaning" in pain and "eagerly" waiting. To the best of my knowledge the earth itself does not actually feel pain and experience futility. However, to make his point, Paul is describing the earth and the things going on in it in human terms. In doing so, he actually compares the concept of a new *earth* to the concept of our new human *bodies*. Paul draws a parallel between the two. He says, "And not *only* the creation, but we ourselves" eagerly await the "redemption of our bodies." Recall in Chapter 7 we described our bodies as new but still somehow related to the old? The Bible uses the analogy of a seed going into the ground and a tree or some other plant coming out (1 Corinthians 15). The seed dies in the comparison but rises to life as a new plant. The seed and the mature plant are quite different but they are actually the same organism. The seed was not completely done away with. The life of the plant was actually in the seed. Likewise, the new earth is new, but not entirely new. There will be continuity between the new earth and the old one–like there will be between our current bodies and our new one–yet it will be new and perfected. The creation will one day experience the same freedom from bondage that we will.

The concept of a suffering earth did not originate in the New Testament. The earth has been suffering and experiencing trials since the first sin. Isaiah took up these themes in a number of passages. Notice a couple of them.

> The earth *mourns and withers*, the world *languishes and withers*, the highest people of the earth languish. The earth lies defiled under its inhabitants; for they have transgressed the laws, violated the statutes, broken the everlasting covenant. Therefore a curse devours the earth, and its inhabitants suffer for their guilt; therefore the inhabitants of the earth are scorched, and few men are left (24:4-6, emphasis added).

> Your dead shall live; their bodies shall rise. You who dwell in the dust, awake and sing for joy! For your dew is a dew of light, and *the earth will give birth to the dead*. Come, my people, enter your chambers, and shut your doors behind you; hide yourselves for a little while until the fury has passed by. For behold, the LORD is coming out from his place to punish the inhabitants of the earth for their iniquity, and the *earth* will disclose the blood shed on it, and *will no more cover its slain* (26:19-21, emphasis added).

The earth mourns and withers. It languishes–so do the people of the earth. See the comparison! The earth and its people suffer alike. The earth suffers because people break God's laws. The curse devours the earth.

Furthermore, the earth is pictured as giving birth to the dead. Women give birth to children. Animals give birth to their young.

But rarely do we think of the earth giving birth to those who have died and been buried. It is ready to spew them out. The term used in the original Greek language for "give birth" is actually a rather violent term. It can mean to "cast out," as if the earth is altogether too eager to get rid of the dead bodies!

Men being buried in the earth is the exact opposite of what God intended at creation. Recall one of God's commands to Adam in the garden was to work to subdue the earth. This means Adam, and all the men after him, were to tame the earth and to make it yield to our purposes. Man was to work the earth, to do what he could to improve upon the natural state of things. He was to cultivate the garden. If he had not eaten the forbidden fruit he would have done these things indefinitely without experiencing death. As it was, however, Adam sinned and death entered the world. When men die, they are buried. Instead of men subduing the earth the earth subdues men. Death is not the original state for man. We ought not to die and be buried in the earth. Things are backward. We know it. The earth is personified as knowing it and not liking it any more than we do. It does not like being used to house dead bodies.

Notice how the earth was being used in the days of Moses. There were several men who had challenged Moses' authority from God. Moses said there would be a test. If the men live a normal length of life and die at a ripe old age then they will not be found guilty in their actions. But if they are guilty, they should expect an entirely different outcome.

> "If the LORD creates something new, and the ground opens its mouth and swallows them up with all that belongs to them, and they go down alive into Sheol, then you shall know that these men have despised the LORD." And as soon as he had finished speaking all these words, the ground under them split apart. And the earth opened its mouth and swallowed them up, with their households and all the people who belonged to Korah and all their goods. So they and all that belonged to them went down alive into Sheol, and the earth closed over them, and they perished from the midst of the assembly (Num. 16:30-33).

It is of course the Lord who opened the earth and caused these men to fall inside and be buried. However, the earth is *pictured* as a monstrous being swallowing men alive! It was not meant to be this way. The earth was created as a lovely garden designed to serve men. Men should have eaten the fruit of the earth–not be eaten by the earth! The land is now "polluted with blood" (Ps. 106:38) that should never have been shed. The earth is being used as a burial cloth to cover the dead (Is. 25:7) who should never have died. Things are backward. They are upside down. We need a new earth because we have spoiled the current one. It needs to be restored to its original condition and relationships to their proper order. Such a day is coming. There will be a day when the earth will no longer cover the dead (Isaiah 26:21). It will be a new earth. An earth suited for Christ and for those who are his.

Application: We tend to love this earth and fear leaving it–but this earth is messed up. Even the earth itself wants to be made new. The biggest problem with this earth is that Christ is not here in his Person as he will be. He is here in Spirit first-fruits, yes, first-fruits and in a very real way. However, we are not with Christ in the sense that Paul longed to be after he died (Philippians 1:23). If we belong to Christ we are not at home here. Our treasure ought not be here. We should feel as if this present earth is not our home. We ought to long for that heavenly city along with Abraham. Do you? Do you feel out of place in this world? Do you long for the presence of Christ and the fellowship with him, the first-fruits or are you comfortable in this broken, messed up world destined for destruction?

CHAPTER 17

Heaven, Part 4:
What Will it be Like?

In the last chapter we discussed the reasons why we need a new earth for Christ and his people. In this chapter, we will focus on understanding what the Bible says about the new earth that we will inherit. We will try to understand what it will look like, what life there will be like, and what we will do. An understanding of these things will hopefully help you to look forward to heaven with joy and eagerness. As we said before, many people have misunderstandings about heaven that keep them from a proper anticipation of it. They think of floating in the clouds, strumming harps, and singing all day. Of course, we will sing in heaven and we will thoroughly love doing so. But this is not all. Unclear, fuzzy thoughts about heaven do not help us look forward to it. These thoughts do not motivate us and fill us with joy. True, accurate thoughts about heaven help us to long for heaven and Christ as we should. With this as our aim, let's begin to consider the new earth.

We have already discussed the problems associated with the current earth. These problems started when Adam sinned and God cursed the troublemaking serpent (Genesis 3:14) and the ground (Genesis 3:17). God's curse against the ground is literally a curse against the earth, the soil under our feet. To help understand what heaven will be like it will be helpful to understand what the earth would have been like without the curse. This is helpful specifically because God has said that in the new earth there will be no curse (Revelation 22:3). The new earth will be like the old earth before the curse. Keeping this in mind, we will look briefly at the original earth, then at the curse.

You will recall that God placed Adam and Eve in a garden. There were all sorts of plants. The plants were for food. There were all sorts of animals as well. Adam did not need to fear the animals. There was no need to kill them either. All of man's dietary needs were met by the food he could easily gather. The animals, even the insects, were no threat to the garden. Adam was simply commanded to work and keep the garden. This would certainly have been an enjoyable garden to work. The plants God placed there were already producing fruit! God had done the work–man just had to keep it going and enjoy the results. All was at peace. Additionally, there were four rivers. One flowed out of the Garden and was placed there specifically to water it. God placed gold and precious stones there. There was a tree of life in the midst of the garden. All was created perfectly and God declared that it was good, even very good.

Then Adam sinned.

After Adam sinned the earth was cursed. Genesis 3:14-24 describes the results of the curse on the ground and on the serpent. These curses impact man and life in this earth in countless ways. We will look at five specific results of the curse as recorded in Genesis 3:14-24.

First, there will be ongoing strife, or fighting between the children of God and the children of the devil (Genesis 3:15). This fighting will continue until the end. While this verse does promise ultimate victory in Christ, it assures us that in the meantime there will be ongoing worldwide conflict. Those who follow God can expect constant opposition at every turn. They can expect the world to hate them and to oppose them. The devil will not be content unless he is causing trouble and opposing God. We can look forward to a world, a new world, in which there are no enemies. God will have no enemies. We will have no enemies.

Second, the woman would have great pain and sorrow in childbirth (Genesis 3:16). I have seen my wife deliver seven children and I can say confidently that there is much pain in childbirth. Much energy and medicine are employed on the part of doctors to help ease the pain. None of this would have been necessary had man not sinned! Imagine a world where there is no such pain! We can look forward to one.

Third, as a result of the curse God caused the ground to bring forth thorns and thistles (Genesis 3:18). These obstacles and the extra work necessary to garden in this new harsh environment would cause Adam pain and sweat (Genesis 3:17,19). The work would no longer be as easy or as fruitful. Adam would have to fight the thorns and other weeds. This would cause sorrow and sweat and consume a considerable amount of time and resources. For most people, even in prosperous countries, we must spend a considerable amount of time working just to produce enough food to eat (whether we grow it ourselves or earn money to purchase it). This is a result of the curse. One day, this task will no longer be opposed by the earth.

Fourth, Adam would experience this extra work and opposition from weeds until he returns to dust (Genesis 3:19). This means he would surely die. Instead of subduing the earth and making it yield its fruit to him, the earth would eventually subdue Adam. His body would wear out and return to the dust from which it was made. Things began to be opposite the way God had created them to be.

Fifth, Adam and Eve were banished from the garden. All their descendants are banished from the garden. A cherub, an angel-like creature, was placed at the gate of the garden with a flaming sword to prevent them from entering in again.

Amazingly, despite our multiplied sins, God has promised to remove the curse and restore the earth to its pristine condition. In describing the new earth God says very clearly and directly in Revelation 22:3 that no longer will anything be accursed. The strife between men will be no more. The sorrow, pain, sweat, opposition from thorns and thistles, and even death will be no more. It may sound to you like God is restoring the earth to a pre-sin Garden of Eden-like condition. It should! This is exactly what the twenty-first and twenty-second chapters of Revelation describe.

Chapter 21 of Revelation pictures the new heaven and new earth as containing a city, *the* city, the heavenly Jerusalem. This is the city Abraham looked forward to. It is beautiful, like a bride prepared for her wedding day, coming down out of heaven (21:2). In his vision John heard a voice from heaven saying that God would now have his dwelling place with men. Recall what we said earlier about heaven being where Christ dwells? Christ is coming to dwell with men on the earth–we will literally experience heaven on earth. He will live with his people in the heavenly city on the new earth.

The new earth is described in terms surprisingly similar to descriptions of the Garden of Eden before Adam sinned. Notice the many similarities that invite comparison. In the new earth there is a river of water, just like in the garden (Revelation 22:1-2, Genesis 2:10). One is called a river of life, the other supplied life-giving water to the garden. There is an emphasis on rare jewels in the heavenly Jerusalem. Notice the comparison to jasper and crystal (Revelation 21:11). The walls and city are built of jasper and pure gold (Revelation 21:18). The walls were decorated with every kind of jewel; many are mentioned (Revelation 21:19-20). You will recall the similar emphases on jewels and precious stones in the garden (Genesis 2:11-12, Ezekiel 28:13). You will see many of the same stones listed. There is also the tree of life in heaven (Revelation 22:2) as was in the garden (Genesis 3:22). Only here we see a sharp contrast. Adam was forbidden to eat from the tree of life after he had sinned. In the new garden, the tree is specifically designated for eating (Revelation 22:14).

The picture of a bride and a holy city coming down from heaven is quite different indeed from being kicked out of a garden. The curse is undone and a joyous celebration ensues. But there is more. God will wipe away every tear. There will be no more mourning, no crying, no pain, and no death (21:4). Can you imagine? No pain of any sort. No physical pain from accidents, illness, insect bites, and scratches. There will be no emotional pain or heartache either. No remorse for things you have done wrong. Your sins will be forgiven and will no longer cause you grief. The old earth on which we currently live will pass away (Revelation 21:1). This age and the wickedness of it will be no more.

The heavenly Jerusalem is not only beautiful and desirable for what it is, but also for what it isn't. In the new city there will be no murderers, no immoral persons, and no one who loves and practices lies and falsehoods. It will be a place for God's people and for them alone. No longer will the wicked persecute the righteous. No longer will God's children be strangers in a foreign land filled with evildoers. It will be their land and their King will be in it with them.

In addition to describing the new earth itself, the Bible gives some indication of what we will do there. Our King will be with us and we will serve him (Revelation 22:3). In fact, we will serve him day and night. We evidently do not get tired of doing this! While we cannot say with certainty everything we will do to serve him we know the word "serve" means to carry out religious duties. This will be a joyful service. There will be no drudgery or unpleasant labor. Recall that Adam was placed in the garden and was to serve the Lord by working the ground. This was before he sinned. It would have been pleasant work. Here, we cannot say for certain that man will work a garden. But we can say that serving may involve what we would call work, pleasant work. We will not be idle. We will be serving One who we love more than we can imagine now. It will be our greatest joy to serve him and know that he is pleased with us.

In heaven, that is, on the new earth, we will see his face (Revelation 22:4). While it evidently remains true that none can see the Father, we will freely and openly see the face of Christ. It will be the most beautiful sight. It will be radiant, so much so that that we will need no lamp or sun in heaven. God will himself be the light (Revelation 22:5). Paul's desire had been to be with Christ (Philippians 1:23). His desire, and hopefully ours, will be ultimately fulfilled in the new heaven and new earth. It will not be a brief meeting followed by a short visit. No, it will be forever. We will enjoy being with the One who loved us and purchased us and rescued us from the well-deserved torments of hell forever. We will see his face and it will be overwhelmingly beautiful.

In addition to being with Christ, we will reign there with him (22:5, 5:10). To reign means to rule or govern. Interestingly, this is the same thing Christ is said to do (Revelation 11:5 and elsewhere). We somehow share in his ruling or governing of the new earth. The Bible does not fully explain how we reign or what authority we will be given but we can conclude that reigning in heaven will certainly be different from the way modern governments reign. We know we will not be involved in law-enforcement type activities since all evildoers will have been banished from the new earth. There will be no crime to punish. There will be no corruption of government officials. There will be no famines or disease outbreaks. No wars. No poverty. No death. Reigning over such a state will be a supreme joy. Christ will be our perfect example and we will have the incredible privilege reigning alongside him.

In addition to reigning, we will rest from our current labors (Revelation 14:13). This may involve physical rest from the physical exertions necessary in this life. However, it probably means more than this. In this life we are to be constantly fighting a spiritual battle against the world, the flesh, and the devil. Temptations abound on every side. The world calls to us to participate in some sinful activity. If we don't fall for one temptation, there is another. If we don't participate in some sin, perhaps we wish we could. We enjoy the idea. We sin with our lips. We sin with our minds. Our flesh tempts us. The devil prowls around like a lion looking for someone to destroy. There is danger to be avoided everywhere we turn. "How can a man keep his way pure?" the Psalmist asks (119:9). By guarding it, he answers. We must constantly be guarding. We must be watching for and fighting against an enemy who would destroy us. We must pray, read Scripture, meditate, fast, seek accountability, and repent of sin. These things take time and they are hard work. Guarding one's heart and working to kill sin in your life should be the Christian's chief employment–this should be your job! Doing this job well is tiring. It will make you weary. It will make you long for a time and place when you no longer have to do these things. The Lord has graciously given us the weekly Sabbath, or Christian Lord's Day every week to rest from our labors and to whet our appetite for heaven. However, Sundays come and go and in between we are back to the battle. We long for a time when we can experience an enduring rest. The age to come is that time. The new heavens and the new earth are that place. There, we rest.

In that time and place we also worship. The fourth chapter of Revelation presents a picture of heaven full of worship. The elders around the throne bow down and cast their crowns before Christ's feet. Living creatures proclaim his holiness. The elders acknowledge his worthiness, power and glory. We also see singing and the use of instruments (5:8). Those worshipping the Lamb seem to be grateful people. There is every indication they enjoy worshipping the Lamb and desire this activity. There is no drudgery in worshipping the Lamb. Those who speak negatively of heaven because they have a low view of worship simply do not understand what it entails. The elders pictured in Revelation 4 are not being forced to do something against their will. They are doing the very thing they most desire to do. Their hearts are full of love and thanksgiving and they are eager to express their feelings for their Savior. The age to come will be a joyous time and place.

In the new heaven and earth we will enjoy rewards. While it is difficult to determine exactly what these rewards will be we can know they will be very good for those who receive them. Paul used the promise of rewards in heaven to motivate his disciples to build their lives on a solid foundation.

> Now if anyone builds on the foundation with gold, silver, precious stones, wood, hay, Straw—each one's work will become manifest, for the Day will disclose it, because it will be revealed by fire, and the fire will test what sort of work each one has done. If the work that anyone has built on the foundation survives, he will receive a reward. If anyone's work is burned up, he will suffer loss, though he himself will be saved, but only as through fire (1 Cor. 3:12-15).

Notice that it is possible to receive a reward for the things you have done. If your work survives you will receive it. This of course means that if your work does not survive you will not receive a reward. It is evidently possible to be saved ("he himself will be saved") but to have all your work burned up and receive no reward. Jesus also taught that by doing good and loving our enemies we should expect a great reward (Luke 6:35). He does not specify exactly what this is, but it is in addition to being "Sons of God." Many books have been written about the nature of the Christian's reward in heaven. Some are helpful, though it is difficult to be certain what is involved since the Bible gives few details. We can be certain, however, that it is a good thing, a thing to be desired, and a thing to motivate us to live the way we ought.

We will evidently enjoy fellowship in heaven. While Christ will be the center of our thoughts and affections, the center of our activities and the focus of our worship, we will also be aware of and apparently enjoy the company of other people. There will be vast numbers of people in heaven. We will retain some or maybe all of our identity. Notice another scene around the throne,

> After this I looked, and behold, a great multitude that no one could number, from every nation, from all tribes and peoples and languages, standing before the throne and before the Lamb, clothed in white robes, with palm branches in their hands, and crying out with a loud voice, "Salvation belongs to our God who sits on the throne, and to the Lamb!" (Revelation 7:9-10).

This vast multitude contained people from every nation, tribe, people group and language. These people retained their national and cultural identity from the old earth. It is almost certain, as we'll see shortly, that they recognized each other and took some pleasure in being together and in being united in what they did. These people from all over the world join together in praising God. They praised God, evidently the Father, and the Lamb. They proclaimed that salvation belongs to our God. There was complete agreement on whose God he is. He was not the God of only the Jews, or only of some race or nation. People from all over the world recognize him as their God and Savior. This is a perfect picture of New Testament fellowship. The word fellowship in the New Testament carries a couple of related but different meanings. One seems to simply be Christians spending meaningful time together in the Lord. This is certainly being done in this scene in heaven! Perhaps in this age fellowship involves visiting, sharing, praying with one another and similar things that benefit Christians. The other meaning has to do with serving Christ and pursuing the cause of the gospel. Fellowship is directly associated with ministering to the saints (2 Corinthians 8:4), the furtherance of the gospel (Philippians 1:3-5), and evangelizing the lost (Galatians 2:9). This meaning is also reflected around the throne in heaven. While the lost will not be in heaven to hear the gospel, it is because of the gospel that any of us will be there. We will be sharing together in the blessings of the gospel–basking in its benefits. We have already noted we serve Christ in heaven. We will do so in the freedom purchased by the gospel in a way we can only approximate in this life.

As mentioned above, we retain our identities. In addition to national and cultural identities, however, we also retain our individual identities. We see this in at least a couple of places in Scripture. One of the sons of King David died when he was only seven days old. David wept bitterly as the child lay dying. After the child died however, David immediately cheered up. When asked why, David gave the following response, "But now he is dead. Why should I fast? Can I bring him back again? I shall go to him, but he will not return to me" (2 Samuel 12:23). David found comfort in the fact that that he could go to be with his son who had just died. David of course was thinking of seeing this son in heaven. The only way this could be comforting however, is if David would recognize his son when he arrived in heaven. He anticipated joy in being reunited.

The apostle Paul also encourages this sort of comfort amidst death. In a verse we have already looked at concerning the second coming, Paul encourages the Thessalonians who have lost loved ones to not grieve and to find comfort in the fact that they will see their Christian family again.

> But we do not want you to be uninformed, brothers, about those who are asleep, that you may not grieve as others do who have no hope. For since we believe that Jesus died and rose again, even so, through Jesus, *God will bring with him those who have fallen asleep.* For this we declare to you by a word from the Lord, that we who are alive, who are left until the coming of the Lord, will not precede

those who have fallen asleep. For the Lord himself will descend from heaven with a cry of command, with the voice of an archangel, and with the sound of the trumpet of God. *And the dead in Christ will rise first.* Then we who are alive, who are left, will be caught up together *with them* in the clouds to meet the Lord in the air, and so we will always be with the Lord. Therefore *encourage one another with these words* (1 Thessalonians 4:13-18, emphasis added).

Paul was writing specifically to encourage these believers who were grieving over loved ones who had died. What encouragement would it be if we saw these loved ones again but did not recognize them? To be meaningful, to enjoy the sort of comfort Paul intends, we must recognize one another in heaven.

Application: Heaven will be wonderful. There, and only there since the fall will we be all that God intended for us to be. We were designed to serve and worship God. We do this so poorly in this life. We will do so perfectly in heaven. There we will serve him in word and song and deed. We will serve him and reign with him in ways we can only dream of. We will do these things with others whom we love and with those we have never even met. The paradise God created in Eden will be restored, complete with rivers and trees and beautiful stones and scenery. We shall do whatever we do there with perfect bodies. We shall do so without the temptation to sin and without the interference of evil persons. The goal of this chapter, and this entire book, is to make you long to be with Christ. You can have a foretaste of this now. You can have your sins forgiven in this life–you can go to him in this life begging for mercy. You can have fellowship and comfort now, in this life. But you can have it so much more in the life to come. Do you desire this? Do you desire to be with Christ now–and one see him day face to face? Do you anxiously await his return? If you do not desire to be with him in the future you must ask yourself if you walk with him even now. Go, seek him out now, and eagerly await his return.